Good and Wholesome

HONEY

Recipes

Good and Wholesome HONEY Recipes

American Honey Institute

Dover Publications, Inc.
New York

Published in Canada by General Publishing Company, Ltd., 30 Lesmill Road, Don Mills, Toronto, Ontario.
Published in the United Kingdom by Constable and Company, Ltd., 10 Orange Street, London WC2H 7EG.

This Dover edition, first published in 1985, is a slightly altered republication of the following two pamphlets:

Old Favorite Honey Recipes, originally published by the American Honey Institute, Madison, Wisconsin, in 1945, as a revised and enlarged edition of the same title originally published in 1941. It corresponds to Part One of the Dover edition.

New Favorite Honey Recipes, originally published by the American Honey Institute in 1947. It corresponds to Part Two of the Dover edition.

The front matter of the Dover edition is a combination of the front matter of the original pamphlets; the index of this edition unites the indexes of the original pamphlets.

Manufactured in the United States of America
Dover Publications, Inc., 31 East 2nd Street, Mineola, N.Y. 11501

Library of Congress Cataloging in Publication Data
Main entry under title:

Good and wholesome honey recipes.

Includes index.
Contents: Old favorite honey recipes — New favorite honey recipes.
1. Cookery (Honey)   I. American Honey Institute.   II. Old favorite honey recipes. 1985.   III. New favorite honey recipes. 1985.
TX767.H7G66   1985   641.6'8   85-6831
ISBN 0-486-24945-X

HONEY

By Dr. Morris Fishbein

MANY CENTURIES have passed since human beings first found that the honey in the combs of the beehive is a useful and pleasant food. The ancient Greeks called it the nectar of the gods. Now that modern medical science and chemistry have been able to analyze honey and to list its constituents we know much more about its nutritional qualities.

Honey is sweet because of its content of sugar. In addition to the sugar, however, it contains many of the minerals which are known to be necessary for the growth and health of the human body. Most of the important constituents of the vitamin B complex are found in honey and also some vitamin C. There are also some hormones and some amino acids.

When ordinary sugar like cane and beet sugar are taken into the body, the digestive processes break them down, as a first step, into the simple sugars called dextrose and levulose. In honey this step has already been accomplished. Absorption of the sugar in honey therefore takes place quickly.

Sugar is the substance from which the human body develops energy. Levulose is twice as sweet as ordinary cane sugar, and its flavor is different. Dextrose is about half as sweet as cane sugar.

Only recently have the nutrition experts studied the vitamin content of honey. These studies were made at the University of Wisconsin. The total vitamin content of honey is not great. The vitamins in honey help to conduct the processes which go on in the body to help it use up the sugar.

The minerals in honey are iron, copper, sodium, potassium, manganese, calcium, magnesium and phosphorus.

Users of honey note that it frequently varies in color. The color is determined by the flowers from which the bees obtain the nectar. White clover honey is greenish yellow while that from buckwheat is a reddish brown.

From "Your Family Doctor" by Dr. Morris Fishbein, by permission of the Chicago Times Syndicate and with permission of Dr. Fishbein.

HONEY HINTS

Honey is a natural, unrefined food. It is unique in that it is the only unmanufactured sweet available in commercial quantities.

Since seventy-five to eighty per cent of its composition is sugars, honey has an energy-producing value second to few foods. Cane and beet sugars must be broken down into simpler sugars by digestive juices before they can be absorbed into the blood stream and assimilated into the tissues. These resulting simple sugars, dextrose and levulose, make up almost the entire sugar content of honey. It has been clinically demonstrated that little digestion is necessary and that absorption takes place quickly.

Honey Puts No Tax Upon Digestive System

The word "sugar" to most people means the sugar of commerce, derived from sugar cane or sugar beets. To the chemist it is the name for a large variety of materials with varying degrees of chemical complexity and great variation in both uses and characteristics. As stated in the preceding paragraph, when ordinary cane sugar is digested, it is split into two simpler sugars, dextrose and levulose. A sugar of this category which splits into two simpler sugars is called a disaccharide. The simple sugars into which it is split are the monosaccharides.

The sugars of honey are primarily monosaccharides, that is, they require no digestive change before they can be absorbed. In honey also may be found small proportions of sucrose (cane sugar), traces of maltose (malt sugar) and sometimes also less well-known sugars. For example, melezitose (a trisaccharide sugar) has been found in some honeydews derived usually from coniferous plants, and sugar alcohols have been found in other honeydews. Naturally, our concern is chiefly with the sugars of honey which occur in amounts large enough to be significant.

Levulose has been called the queen of sugars. It is almost twice as sweet as cane sugar, and, besides its sweetness, it carries to the human senses something that might almost be called a flavor. In a pure state this sugar is difficult to obtain, but it occurs naturally in mixtures with other sugars not only in honey but in many fruits. It dissolves in water readily and when dissolved it crystallizes out only under circumstances that are difficult to produce, so that if one finds crystals in honey they are not crystals of levulose but of dextrose.

Dextrose (sometimes also called "d-glucose" but not to be confused with commercial glucose syrup) is a sugar of quite different nature. It is almost half as sweet as cane sugar, dissolves in about its own weight of water at ordinary temperatures, and crystallizes from a water solution quickly when it occurs in more than an amount equal to the water of solution. It is this sugar in honey that forms crystals. It should be noted that in an average honey the percent of dextrose is roughly twice the percent of water, hence we may expect that on standing, dextrose crystals will be thrown down. It is because of this that honeys granulate.

If crystals form in honey quickly, they are usually small, whereas if they form slowly, they are coarse. These differences involve no chemical differences, only a difference in the size of the crystals. On the market we find specially processed finely crystalline honey of smooth texture.

In addition to its sugars, honey contains as its minor components a considerable number of mineral constituents, seven members of the B vitamin complex, ascorbic acid (vitamin C), dextrins, plant pigments, amino acids and other organic acids, traces of protein, esters and other aromatic compounds, and several enzymes.

The Average Chemical Composition of Honey

The Principal Components	Percent
Water	17.7
Levulose (fruit sugar)	40.5
Dextrose (grape sugar)	34.0
Sucrose (cane sugar)	1.9
Dextrins and gums	1.5
Ash (Silica, Iron, Copper, Manganese, Chlorine, Calcium, Potassium, Sodium, Phosphorus, Sulfur, Aluminum, Magnesium)	0.18
Total	95.78

Known Substances Difficult to Demonstrate Quantitatively:
Enzymes:
  Invertase (converts sucrose to dextrose and levulose), Diastase (converts starch to maltose), Catalase (decomposes hydrogen peroxide), Inulase (converts inulin to levulose)
Aromatic bodies (terpenes, aldehydes, esters)
Higher alcohols (mannitol, dulcitol, etc.)
Maltose, rare sugars (sometimes melezitose, etc.)

In every 100 grams of honey there are 0.18 of a gram of mineral constituents.

Honey Contains Vitamins

The vitamin content of honey about which there has been much discussion has recently been under laboratory study. Many of the earlier workers reported the absence of vitamins. This is not surprising since many foods relatively low in vitamins were given a similar rating because the then-available methods did not detect small quantities of the vitamins. With the present improved procedures the vitamin content of any food material can be estimated with considerable accuracy. Extensive studies on the B vitamin content of honey have recently been made by Kitzes, Schuette, and Elvehjem.*

While it is true that honey cannot be regarded as a real source of vitamins, on the other hand, it is not devoid of these dietary essentials. This means that when honey is consumed, it supplies, in small part, the vitamins needed for the metabolism of the sugar ingested from the honey. Since many of the B vitamins are used in the metabolism of sugar, we can calculate what part of the total require-

*Kitzes, George, Schuette, H. A., Elvehjem, C. A., The Vitamins in Honey. Journal of Nutrition 26 No. 3: 241–250, 1943.

ment honey supplies for its metabolism by the body. It is found that honey supplies approximately $1/25$ of the thiamine needed for utilization of its carbohydrate. Likewise the amount of riboflavin found in honey provides about $1/8$ and the niacin $1/10$ of the quantity required for metabolism of the sugar. Similar calculations cannot be made for pantothenic acid, pyridoxine and biotin because the requirements for human beings are not known, but small amounts of each of these vitamins are present in honey.

Honey Contains Minerals

Among the mineral elements found in honey are iron, copper, sodium, potassium, manganese, calcium, magnesium and phosphorus. These minerals are all essential to good nutrition of animals. They are all present in honey, although in some cases only in trace quantities.

Honey and Infants

Honey is a pleasant, safe source of readily available energy for adults and for children who are more than one year old. However, the United States Food and Drug Administration and other health-related organizations have issued recent warnings about the possible harmful effects honey can have on infants less than a year old. Studies have shown that honey ingested by young babies can, in some cases, cause infant botulism. Consult your physician for further information.

Types of Honey

Honey is available the year around and may be purchased in various forms. It is on the market in liquid, comb, chunk, cut comb, solid, sometimes called granulated or finely crystallized, and creamed honey, a finely crystallized honey of creamy consistency.

To Purchase Honey

Select the flavor you desire. The flavor depends upon the kind of flowers from which the bees gather nectar. Honey producers frequently mix several honeys by heating moderately and stirring to produce a blend with a flavor that is most satisfactory.

To Store Honey

Keep liquid honey in a dry place. Freezing does not injure the color or flavor but may hasten granulation. Avoid damp places for storage because honey has the property of absorbing and retaining moisture. Do not put honey in the refrigerator.

To Liquefy Honey That Has Granulated or Solidified

Place the container in a bowl of warm water—not warmer than the hand can bear—until all crystals are melted. See that the honey container does not rest on the bottom of the water container.

To Serve Honey

You may secure a honey container with a top that cuts the flow of honey and leaves no drip or stickiness. Individual containers are liked by children.

To Use Honey in the Freezing of Fruits

Use a light-flavored honey. For sliced or crushed fruits, use 1 part of honey to 4 or 5 parts fruit. For whole fruits, add 1 cup water to each 2 cups honey. Use just enough of this diluted honey to cover the fruit.

To Replace Sugar in Cakes and Cookies

A general rule is to reduce the amount of liquid ¼ cup for each cup of honey used to replace sugar.

Cakes and cookies made with honey are noted for their keeping qualities. The ability of honey to absorb and retain moisture and thus retard the drying out and staling of baked goods is of great importance to homemakers who wish to do their baking in advance. This property combined with the food value and flavor of honey is valuable also to the baker.

To Measure Honey

Measure shortening first, and then measure honey in the same measuring unit.

Weight of Honey

A cup of honey weighs 12 ounces of which not quite ⅕ is moisture. This yields approximately 9¼ ounces of carbohydrate as compared with the 7 ounces contained in a cup of sugar. Honey contains more carbohydrate than the same measure of cane sugar.

To Cook with Honey

1. Read the recipe carefully.
2. Assemble all ingredients and utensils before starting to mix.
3. Grease pans that are to be greased.
4. Measure ingredients accurately with standard measuring cups and measuring spoons.
5. Follow directions in recipe.
6. Sift flour once before measuring. Pile lightly in standard measuring cup (do not shake down), level off with straight edge of knife.
7. Flour containing husks or bran coats like cornmeal, graham, or bran are mixed in, not sifted.
8. Use amount of baking powder that directions on baking powder container specify.
9. The amount of soda needed to neutralize the acidity in one cup of the average honey is $1/12$ to $1/5$ teaspoon. When sour milk and honey appear in a recipe, it is not necessary to add any extra soda for the honey.
10. Unless specified, the honey is in liquid form. Granulated and creamed honey may be used with equal success in any combination that is heated.

The Following Amounts Will Serve Approximately 40 Persons

1 pound coffee
1 quart cream
1 pound honey—
    will sweeten coffee for 40
10 quarts milk
1 pound butter or margarine
1 quart honey French dressing
1 peck potatoes
2 10-pound honey-baked hams
80 honey rolls
2 quarts sandwich filling
6 quarts salad
6 pounds cabbage (for salad)

1 quart honey mayonnaise
5 pounds dried beans
2 quarts olives
2 gallons honey ice cream
4 9-inch honey layer cakes
    (serves 40 generously)
2 dozen medium-sized lemons
2 pounds honey
8 quarts water
    (makes honey lemonade for 40)
3 pints honey jam
1 peck sweet potatoes

Useful Equivalents

	approximately
2 cups fat	1 pound
2¼ cups brown sugar, firmly packed	1 pound
3½ cups confectioners' sugar	1 pound
4 cups flour (sifted)	1 pound
4½ cups cake flour (sifted)	1 pound
3½ cups graham flour	1 pound
½ cup evaporated milk and ½ cup water	1 cup milk
8 to 10 egg whites	1 cup egg whites
1 square unsweetened chocolate	1 ounce
3½ tablespoons cocoa and ½ tablespoon butter	1 square chocolate
1 tablespoon cornstarch	2 tablespoons flour (thickening)
4 to 5 lemons	1 cup juice
1 pound peanut butter	1⅔ cups
14 to 16 slices bacon	1 pound
2½ cups raisins	1 pound
1 cup raw rice	3 cups cooked
1 package macaroni (8 oz.)	4 cups cooked
2½ cups dates	1 pound
3 cups figs (chopped)	1 pound
3½ cups walnuts (chopped)	1 pound

Favorite Ways to Use Honey au naturel

SUNDAY   Hot biscuits and honey for breakfast
Waffles with warm honey for supper

EVERY DAY   Cereal with honey
Fruit with honey
Bread and butter with honey
Milk and honey for a nutritious and tasty beverage

Honey Hints

PART ONE

Old Favorite Honey Recipes

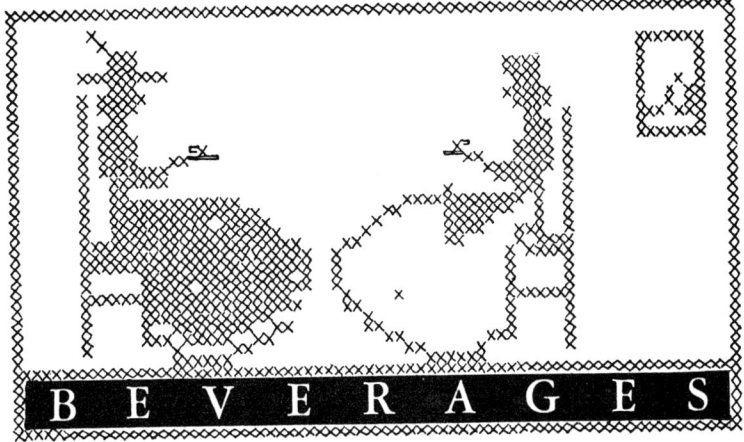

BEVERAGES

*"A drink that tastes of honey sweet
Will always make a gracious treat."*

Coffee

(medium strong)
2 level tablespoons coffee
1 cup boiling water

(strong)
3 level tablespoons coffee
1 cup boiling water

Put the coffee into the pot with a little egg white or a crushed egg shell. Add a little cold water and stir all together thoroughly. Measure boiling water and add to the coffee. Place over the heat for three minutes. Turn off heat and let settle. Serve with honey.

Tea

Scald a china or earthen teapot. Allow one teaspoon of tea to each cup of freshly-boiled water. Pour boiling water over tea. Allow to steep 3 minutes. Serve at once with honey.

Honey Cocoa Sirup

1¼ cup cocoa
1 cup sugar
½ teaspoon salt
⅛ teaspoon ground allspice
⅛ teaspoon ground cinnamon
1½ cups boiling water
½ cup honey
2 teaspoons vanilla extract

Combine cocoa, sugar, salt, and spices. Add boiling water. Blend. Place over low heat, bring to a boil and boil 5 minutes, stirring constantly. Remove from fire. Cool. Add honey and vanilla. Store in covered jar in refrigerator until ready to use. Approximate yield: 2¼ cups.
To serve: Heat ¼ cup Honey Cocoa Sirup with 2 cups scalded milk over boiling water. Before serving, beat with rotary beater. Yield: 3 servings. Honey gives this sirup an unusual smoothness and a delicious flavor in addition to extra food value.

Lemonade

Mix 2 tablespoons of honey with the juice of ½ lemon. Stir well. Add 1 cup hot or cold water according to whether hot or cold drink is desired.

Russian Tea (45 cups)

1 box stick cinnamon (1¼ ounces)
1 box whole cloves (1¼ ounces)
¾ cup honey
3 oranges, juice of 3 and grated rind of 1
6 lemons, juice of 6 and grated rind of 1
⅛ cup black tea
5 quarts water, boiling

Cook spices, honey and grated rind with 2 cups water for 10 minutes. Let stand 1 hour. Strain. Steep tea in the boiling water 1 minute. Then add fruit juice and spice mixture. Serve hot.

Refreshing Party Drink

1 quart currants
1 pint water
1 cup honey
1 small stick cinnamon
5 oranges
3 lemons
water

Wash currants, place in a kettle and cover with water. Reserve ¼ cup currants for garnishing. Simmer gently for 10 minutes. Strain. If a clear juice is desired, do not press the pulp. Combine the pint of water, honey, and cinnamon and boil for 5 minutes. Remove the spice stick. Combine the juice of the oranges, lemons, and currant juice with the spiced sirup, diluted to taste. Fresh pineapple or cranberry juice may be used instead of orange and lemon juice. Serve hot or cold.

Grape Juice

Mix 2 tablespoons honey with ¼ cup of boiling water. Stir until dissolved. Add enough hot grape juice to fill glass. 2 tablespoons of lemon juice may be added for variety. This makes a delicious cold weather drink.

Milk

For extra flavor and nourishment add 2 tablespoons of honey to a glass of milk. Serve hot or cold.

Honey Eggnog

4 to 6 egg yolks
4 tablespoons honey
4 cups milk
nutmeg

Beat the yolks of eggs until lemon colored. Add honey and mix well. Add milk slowly. Fill glasses. Add a slight grating of nutmeg. Serve at once.

To make an Orange Eggnog, replace milk with orange juice. Omit nutmeg.

BREADS

*"If I had all of Croesus' money
I'd still subsist on bread and honey."*

Enriched Bread (2 loaves)

2 cups milk or 1 cup milk and 1 cup water

1 tablespoon salt

2 tablespoons shortening

2 tablespoons honey

1 cake compressed or dry granular yeast

6 cups enriched flour (about)

Scald milk and cool to lukewarm. Add salt and shortening. Put honey and yeast in mixing bowl; let stand until yeast is softened. Add milk and half the flour. Beat thoroughly. Gradually add enough flour to make a soft dough. Turn out on floured board and knead until smooth and elastic. This requires about 8 minutes. Place in slightly-greased bowl and let rise until double in bulk. Punch down lightly and let rise again. Form into loaves. Place in greased pans. Allow to rise until double in bulk. If baked in individual loaves (one pound), bake 40 minutes at 400–425° F.

Whole Wheat Bread (2 loaves)

2 cups milk or 1 cup milk and 1 cup water

1 tablespoon salt

¼ cup shortening

¼ cup honey

1 cake compressed or dry granular yeast

5½ cups (about) whole wheat flour, finely ground

Scald milk and cool to lukewarm. Add salt and shortening. Put honey and yeast in mixing bowl; let stand until yeast is softened. Add milk and 2 cups whole wheat flour. Beat thoroughly. Add another cup of flour and beat again. Add remainder of flour. Turn out on floured board and knead until no longer sticky. This requires about 8 minutes. Place in slightly-greased bowl and let rise until double in bulk. Punch down lightly and let rise again. Shape into two loaves and place in greased pans. Let rise until double in bulk. Bake at 375° F. for about 50 minutes or until nicely browned and loaf begins to shrink from the pan. Keep dough at even temperature (85° F.) for rising.

Honey Oatmeal Bread (3 loaves)

- 1½ cups milk
- 1 cup quick cooking oatmeal
- 2 tablespoons shortening
- 1 can evaporated milk (13 oz. size)
- ¼ cup honey
- 1 tablespoon salt
- 1 or 2 cakes compressed or dry granular yeast
- 2 cups flour
- 3 cups whole wheat flour (about)

Boil milk, add oatmeal, and cook 2 minutes. Add shortening. When melted, add evaporated milk, honey and salt. Cool to lukewarm (98° F.), add crumbled yeast and let stand 2 minutes. Add flour and beat well. Add whole wheat flour to form a soft dough. Knead until mixture is smooth (about 8 minutes). Let rise until double in bulk, form into 3 loaves. Let loaves rise until double in bulk, and bake at 375° F. for 45–50 minutes.

Orange Nut Bread

- 2 tablespoons shortening
- 1 cup honey
- 1 egg
- 1½ tablespoons grated orange rind
- ¾ cup orange juice
- 2¼ cups flour
- 2½ teaspoons baking powder
- ⅛ teaspoon soda
- ½ teaspoon salt
- ¾ cup chopped nut meats

Cream the shortening and honey well. Add the beaten egg and orange rind. Sift the dry ingredients and add alternately with the orange juice. Add chopped nuts. Pour into greased loaf pan, the bottom of which has been lined with waxed paper. Bake at 325° F. for 1 hour or until the loaf is nicely browned and begins to shrink from the pan. Yield: 1 loaf.

Nut Bread

- ½ cup shortening
- ½ cup sugar
- ½ cup honey
- 1 egg
- 3 cups sifted flour
- 3 teaspoons baking powder
- 1 teaspoon salt
- ¾ cup milk
- 1 cup chopped nuts

Cream together shortening and sugar. Add honey and mix thoroughly. Add egg, beating well. Sift together flour, baking powder, and salt. Add to creamed mixture alternately with milk. Add nuts. Bake in greased loaf pan in moderate oven (350° F.) 1¼ hours. Yield: 1 loaf.

Corn Bread

- ¾ cup cornmeal
- 1 cup flour
- 3 teaspoons baking powder
- ½ teaspoon salt
- 1 cup milk
- ¼ cup honey
- 1 egg
- 2 tablespoons melted butter

Mix dry ingredients. Add milk, honey, and beaten egg. Add melted butter last. Bake 25 minutes in a buttered shallow pan in hot oven (400°F.). Serve with honey.

Honey Currant Cake

1 cake compressed or dry granular yeast
¼ cup lukewarm water
½ cup milk
¼ cup honey
1 teaspoon salt
¼ cup melted shortening
1 egg
2 cups sifted enriched flour (about)
½ cup currants

Soften yeast in lukewarm water. Scald milk and cool to lukewarm. Add honey, salt, shortening. Beat egg and add. Blend thoroughly. Add 1 cup flour and beat well. Add softened yeast. Add currants and remaining flour to make a moderately stiff drop batter. Beat until smooth. Cover and let rise until bubbly (about 1 hour). Stir down, pour into greased pan 8 x 8 x 2-inches, filling pan about half full. Spread batter with honey (4 tablespoons). Sprinkle ¼ teaspoon cinnamon and ¼ cup chopped nuts over honey. Let rise until double in bulk. Bake in moderate oven (375° F.) 35 to 40 minutes. (May also be baked as muffins, 20 to 25 minutes). Yield: 1 cake, 8 x 8-inches, or 1½ dozen 2-inch muffins.

Refrigerator Rolls

½ cup honey
1 cake compressed or dry granular yeast
½ cup mashed potatoes
2 cups milk and potato water
1 tablespoon salt
5 cups flour (about)
½ cup melted shortening

Combine honey and yeast and let stand to soften yeast. Add mashed potatoes to scalded milk and water. Cool to lukewarm. Combine yeast and liquid mixture. Add salt, half the flour, and beat thoroughly. Add melted shortening and remainder of flour to make a soft dough. Knead. Let rise until double in bulk. Punch down, and put in a cold place for 24 hours or more, or shape at once, and put in a warm place to rise. Bake at 425° F. for 15 to 20 minutes. Note: If dough in refrigerator rises, punch down. This dough will keep 4 or 5 days.
Put 3 small balls of dough in greased muffin pans for clover leaf rolls.

Pecan Rolls

½ cup butter or margarine
1 cup honey
1 cup pecan halves
sweet roll dough

When sweet dough is light, punch down and let rest a few minutes. Roll out in sheet one-half inch thick. Brush with butter and spread with honey. Roll as a jelly roll and seal edge firmly. Cut into one-inch slices. In bottom of the baking pan place butter cut into small pieces. Spread honey over this and scatter on the pecans. Place rolls one inch apart on the honey and butter mixture. Cover and let rise until double in bulk. Bake in moderate oven (375° F.) 20 to 25 minutes. Let rolls stand in pans one minute after baking before turning them out. If greased muffin pans are used, place ½ teaspoon butter and 1 teaspoon honey in each muffin cup.

Sweet Rolls

1 cup milk
¼ cup honey
¼ cup shortening
1 teaspoon salt
2 cakes compressed or dry granular yeast
¼ cup lukewarm water
2 eggs
5 cups flour (about)

Scald milk. Add honey, shortening, and salt. Soften yeast in lukewarm water and add to milk mixture. Add beaten eggs and half the flour. Beat well. Add rest of flour. Mix well. Knead on a slightly-floured board until smooth. Place in slightly-greased bowl. Cover and let rise until double in bulk. Punch down and form into rolls or coffee cake. Let rise again. Bake at 400–425° F. 20–25 minutes.

Honey Rolls

1 cup milk
¼ cup shortening
½ cup honey
1 cake compressed or dry granular yeast softened in ¼ cup lukewarm water
1½ teaspoons salt
4 cups flour
1 egg

Scald milk, add shortening and honey, cool to lukewarm. Add yeast, salt and 2 cups of flour. Add beaten egg and remainder of flour to form a soft dough. Knead lightly until smooth. Let rise twice, then form into rolls. Let rolls rise until light. Bake at 400° F. about 20 minutes.

Quick Coffee Cake

1½ cups sifted flour
2 teaspoons baking powder
½ teaspoon salt
1 egg
⅔ cup milk
⅓ cup honey
3 tablespoons melted shortening

Sift together dry ingredients. Beat egg. Add milk, honey, and melted shortening. Stir into dry ingredients. Mix lightly (only enough to moisten flour). Spread in lightly greased 8-inch square pan. Cover batter with Honey Topping. Bake in hot oven (400° F.) 25 to 30 minutes.

Honey Topping

¼ cup butter or margarine
¼ cup sugar
¼ cup sifted flour
¼ cup honey
¼ cup chopped nuts

Cream butter or margarine. Add sugar, flour, and honey and mix thoroughly. Sprinkle with nut meats.

Waffles

2 cups flour
3 teaspoons baking powder
½ teaspoon salt
1½ cups milk
2 tablespoons honey
2 eggs
½ cup melted shortening

Sift dry ingredients. Combine milk, honey, egg yolks, shortening, and add to dry ingredients. Fold in stiffly beaten egg whites. Bake in hot waffle iron.
Serve with the following: Heat 1 cup honey in top of double boiler. Add ⅛ to ¼ cup butter and ¼ teaspoon cinnamon, if desired. Serve warm.

Honey French Toast

2 eggs
1 pint milk
¼ cup honey
½ teaspoon salt
a sprinkling of mace or nutmeg
6 or 8 slices of bread several days old

Beat eggs until light. Warm the milk slightly and blend well with the honey. Add the salt, mace, and beaten eggs and stir well. Cut bread about one-half inch thick. Dip each slice into the milk and egg mixture and place on a hot well-greased griddle. Brown well on both sides. Serve with honey.

Honey Milk Toast

2 cups hot milk
½ teaspoon salt
1 tablespoon butter
6 slices buttered toast

Spread each slice of buttered hot toast with honey. Heat milk just to the boiling point, add salt and butter. Keep hot until ready to serve and then pour over the honey spread toast. Serve at once before toast loses its crispness.

Honey Cinnamon Toast

Toast slices of bread on one side. While still hot, butter the untoasted side of bread. Spread buttered side with honey. Sprinkle cinnamon over the top. Place slices under broiler flame until the bread is well browned and the dressing is well blended.

Honey Orange Muffins

½ cup sifted flour
½ teaspoon salt
2 teaspoons baking powder
½ cup whole wheat flour
1 egg, well beaten
¼ cup orange juice
1 teaspoon grated orange rind
½ cup honey
3 tablespoons melted shortening

Sift flour, salt, and baking powder together. Add whole wheat flour and mix thoroughly. Combine egg, orange juice and rind, honey, and shortening. Add all at once to flour, stirring only enough to dampen all flour. Bake in well-greased muffin pans in moderately hot oven (400° F.) 15 to 20 minutes, or until browned.

Breads 9

Corn Muffins

¾ cup sifted flour
1¼ teaspoons baking powder
½ teaspoon salt
⅛ cup cornmeal
¼ cup prepared apple
1 egg, well beaten
⅓ cup milk
¼ cup honey
3 tablespoons shortening, melted

Sift flour once, measure, add baking powder and salt, and sift again. Add cornmeal. Wash, pare, and cut apples into eighths. Remove core and cut crosswise into very thin slices. Combine egg, milk, honey, and shortening. Add all at once to flour-cornmeal mixture, stirring only enough to dampen all flour. Fold in apple. Bake in well-greased 2-inch muffin pans in hot oven (400° F.) for 20 minutes, or until done. Approximate yield: 8–12 muffins.

Bran Raisin Muffins

1 cup flour
4 teaspoons baking powder
½ teaspoon salt
¾ cup bran
½ cup seeded raisins
½ cup milk
4 tablespoons honey
2 tablespoons shortening, melted
1 egg, beaten

Sift flour, baking powder, and salt together; stir in bran and add raisins. Combine the milk, honey, melted shortening, and beaten egg. Add dry ingredients. Stir just enough to moisten the flour. Pour into greased muffin pans and bake in moderately hot oven at 425° F. for 25 minutes.

Honey Muffins with Variations

2 cups flour
1 teaspoon salt
3 teaspoons baking powder
1 cup milk
4 tablespoons honey
1 egg, beaten
¼ cup melted shortening

Sift flour with salt and baking powder. Mix milk, honey, beaten egg, and melted shortening. Add to dry mixture. Stir quickly just long enough to moisten dry ingredients. Fill greased muffin pans one-half full. Bake in a moderately hot oven (400° F.) 25 to 30 minutes or until delicately browned.

Variations

BLUEBERRY MUFFINS — Add ½ cup fresh blueberries to sifted dry ingredients.

FRUIT MUFFINS — Add ½ cup chopped citron, ¼ cup chopped maraschino cherries to batter. Brush muffins lightly with honey before baking.

HONEY MUFFINS — Put 1 teaspoon finely crystallized honey in center of batter of each muffin.

PEANUT BUTTER MUFFINS — Blend ¼ cup peanut butter with honey before adding to milk and egg mixture.

SOYBEAN MUFFINS — Replace ½ cup flour with ½ cup soybean flour.

WHOLE WHEAT MUFFINS — Replace 1 cup of flour with 1 cup of whole wheat flour.

CAKES

*"With butter, egg and good honey
Your cake will moist and flaky be."*

Honey Angel Food

1 teaspoon cream of tartar
½ teaspoon salt
1 cup egg whites (8 to 10 whites)
¾ cup sugar
1 cup cake flour
½ cup honey
½ teaspoon grated lemon rind

Add the cream of tartar and salt to the egg whites in a bowl. Beat the whites with a wire whip until they are stiff. They should move only slightly when the bowl is tipped. Fold one half the sugar slowly into the egg whites 2 tablespoons at a time. Sift the remaining sugar with the flour and add later. The ½ cup honey must be warmed so that it will be thin and will pour in a fine stream over the egg whites as the egg whites are folded in. After the honey is added, fold in the flour and sugar mixture, sifting ¼ cup over the whites at a time. Add grated lemon rind. Pour the mixture into an angel food pan and bake at a temperature of 300° F. for 50 minutes. Invert the pan, cool and remove to a cake rack.

Chocolate Honey Angel Food Cake

¾ cup sifted cake flour
¼ cup cocoa
1 cup sifted granulated sugar
1 cup egg whites (8 to 10 whites)
¼ teaspoon salt
¾ teaspoon cream of tartar
1 teaspoon vanilla extract
⅛ cup honey

Sift flour once, measure, add cocoa and ¼ cup of the sugar, and sift together 4 times. Beat egg whites and salt with rotary beater or flat wire whisk. When foamy, add cream of tartar and vanilla. Continue beating until eggs are stiff enough to hold up in peaks, but not dry. Add remaining ¾ cup of sugar, 2 tablespoons at a time, beating after each addition until sugar is just blended. Add honey, 2 tablespoons at a time, beating after each addition until honey is just blended. Sift about ¼ cup flour-sugar mixture over egg whites and fold in lightly; repeat until all flour is used. Turn into ungreased angel food pan. Cut gently through batter with knife to remove air bubbles. Bake in slow oven (325° F.) 1 hour. Remove from oven and invert pan 1 hour, or until cold.

Super Delicious Chocolate Cake

- 3 squares unsweetened chocolate, melted
- ⅔ cup honey
- 1¾ cups sifted cake flour
- 1 teaspoon soda
- ¾ teaspoon salt
- ½ cup butter or other shortening
- ½ cup sugar
- 1 teaspoon vanilla extract
- 2 eggs, unbeaten
- ⅔ cup water

Blend chocolate and honey; cool to lukewarm. Sift flour once, measure, add soda and salt, and sift together three times. Cream butter thoroughly, add sugar gradually, and cream together until light and fluffy. Add chocolate-honey mixture and vanilla. Blend. Add eggs, one at a time, beating thoroughly after each addition. Add flour, alternately with water, a small amount at a time, beating after each addition until smooth. Bake in two greased 8-inch layer pans in moderate oven (350° F.) 30 to 35 minutes. Spread with French Honey-Chocolate Frosting.

French Honey-Chocolate Frosting

- ½ cup sugar
- ¼ cup butter
- ¼ cup light cream
- ¼ cup honey
- ¼ teaspoon salt
- 3 squares unsweetened chocolate, cut into small pieces
- 2 egg yolks, well beaten

Combine sugar, butter, cream, honey, salt, and chocolate in top of double boiler. Place over boiling water. When chocolate is melted, beat with rotary beater until blended. Pour small amount of mixture over egg yolks, stirring vigorously. Return to double boiler and cook 2 minutes longer, or until mixture thickens slightly, stirring constantly. Remove from hot water, place in pan of ice water or cracked ice, and beat until of right consistency to spread. Yield: Frosting to cover tops and sides of 2 (8-inch) layers.

Orange Honey Cake

- 2 cups sifted cake flour
- 3½ teaspoons baking powder
- ¾ teaspoon salt
- ½ cup butter or other shortening
- ½ cup sugar
- ⅔ cup honey
- 2 egg yolks
- ½ cup orange juice
- 2 egg whites, stiffly beaten

Sift flour once, measure, add baking powder and salt, and sift together three times. Cream butter thoroughly, add sugar gradually, and cream together until light and fluffy. Add honey. Blend. Add egg yolks and beat thoroughly. Add flour, alternately with orange juice, a small amount at a time, beating after each addition until smooth. Fold in egg whites. Bake in two greased 9-inch layer pans in moderate oven (350° F.) 30 to 35 minutes.

Boiled Honey Frosting

- 1½ cups honey
- ⅛ teaspoon salt
- 2 egg whites

Cook honey and salt to 238° F. or until it will spin a thread, or make a soft ball when dropped into cold water. Beat egg whites. Pour the hot honey in a thin stream over the beaten egg whites continuing to beat until all honey is added and frosting will stand in peaks. Spread on cake.

Honey Ginger Cake

2½ cups sifted cake flour
1 teaspoon soda
½ teaspoon baking powder
1 teaspoon salt
1 teaspoon ground ginger
1 teaspoon ground cinnamon
½ cup butter
½ cup brown sugar, firmly packed
1 egg, unbeaten
1 cup honey
1 cup sour milk or buttermilk

Sift flour once, measure, add soda, baking powder, salt, and spices, and sift together three times. Cream butter thoroughly, add sugar gradually, and cream together until light and fluffy. Add egg and beat thoroughly. Add honey and blend. Add flour, alternately with sour milk, a small amount at a time, beating after each addition until smooth. Bake in two well-greased 9-inch layer pans in moderate oven (350° F.) 45 minutes or until done.
Note: If baked in paper-lined cup cake pans, bake at 350° F, for 30 minutes.

Uncooked Honey Frosting

⅛ teaspoon salt
1 egg white
½ cup honey
½ teaspoon flavoring

Add salt to egg white. Warm honey over hot water. Pour in a thin stream over egg white while beating vigorously. Add flavoring. Continue to beat until thick and fluffy.

Frosting with Chopped Apricots

To boiled Honey Frosting add ⅔ cup of well washed, chopped dried apricots. Add ¼ teaspoon each of almond and lemon extract. This frosting gives a new flavor to a light cake.

Honey Fruit Cake

2 cups butter or other shortening
1½ cups brown sugar
1 cup honey
9 eggs
4 cups flour
1 teaspoon soda
1 teaspoon cinnamon
1 teaspoon mace
3 tablespoons milk
2 pounds seeded raisins
2 pounds currants
1 pound nut meats (almonds if available)
1 pound candied citron
1 pound candied orange
1 pound candied lemon
candied cherries and candied rhubarb if desired

Cream butter, add sugar and honey and cream well. Add well beaten eggs, flour, soda and spices that have been sifted together. Add milk. Add the slightly floured fruit that has been carefully washed and dried in oven, almonds that have been blanched and dried, candied fruit cut in pieces. Mix well and place in pans that have been lined with greased brown paper. Decorate top of cake with cherries, almonds and strips of citron. Place greased paper over top of cake. Steam for 2½ hours and then bake in a slow oven (250°F.) for 2½ hours.

Cakes 13

Honey Layer Cake

½ cup shortening
½ cup sugar
½ cup honey
2 egg yolks
2 cups sifted cake flour
3 teaspoons baking powder
¾ teaspoon salt
¾ cup milk
½ teaspoon flavoring
2 egg whites

Cream shortening thoroughly. Add sugar and honey, beat until mixture is light and fluffy. Add egg yolks and beat well. Add sifted dry ingredients alternately with milk. Add flavoring and fold in stiffly-beaten egg whites. Bake in 2 layers at 350° F. for 30 minutes.

Note: Spread Lemon, Fig, or Orange Filling between layers. If you desire a Chocolate Flake Cake, fold in with the beaten egg whites 1 cup chocolate flakes made by cutting unsweetened chocolate finely, or putting chocolate through meat grinder.

Lemon Filling

¼ cup sugar
2 tablespoons flour
¼ cup lemon juice
½ cup honey
    grated rind of 1 lemon
1 egg, slightly beaten
1 tablespoon butter

Mix ingredients in top of double boiler. Cook over hot water, stirring constantly until thickened. Cool. Spread between layers of cake.

Fig Filling

½ cup chopped figs
½ cup honey
¼ cup water
2 tablespoons orange juice
1 tablespoon corn starch

Mix ingredients in top of double boiler and cook until thick enough to spread. Spread between cake layers while hot.

Orange Filling

2 tablespoons sugar
2 tablespoons flour
½ tablespoon lemon juice
½ cup orange juice
¼ cup honey
    grated rind of 1 orange
1 egg, slightly beaten
1 tablespoon butter

Mix ingredients in top of double boiler and cook until thickened. Cool and spread between cake layers.

Honey Ginger Cake

2½ cups sifted cake flour
1 teaspoon soda
½ teaspoon baking powder
1 teaspoon salt
1 teaspoon ground ginger
1 teaspoon ground cinnamon
½ cup butter
½ cup brown sugar, firmly packed
1 egg, unbeaten
1 cup honey
1 cup sour milk or buttermilk

Sift flour once, measure, add soda, baking powder, salt, and spices, and sift together three times. Cream butter thoroughly, add sugar gradually, and cream together until light and fluffy. Add egg and beat thoroughly. Add honey and blend. Add flour, alternately with sour milk, a small amount at a time, beating after each addition until smooth. Bake in two well-greased 9-inch layer pans in moderate oven (350° F.) 45 minutes or until done.
Note: If baked in paper-lined cup cake pans, bake at 350° F, for 30 minutes.

Uncooked Honey Frosting

⅛ teaspoon salt
1 egg white
½ cup honey
½ teaspoon flavoring

Add salt to egg white. Warm honey over hot water. Pour in a thin stream over egg white while beating vigorously. Add flavoring. Continue to beat until thick and fluffy.

Frosting with Chopped Apricots

To boiled Honey Frosting add ⅔ cup of well washed, chopped dried apricots. Add ¼ teaspoon each of almond and lemon extract. This frosting gives a new flavor to a light cake.

Honey Fruit Cake

2 cups butter or other shortening
1½ cups brown sugar
1 cup honey
9 eggs
4 cups flour
1 teaspoon soda
1 teaspoon cinnamon
1 teaspoon mace
3 tablespoons milk
2 pounds seeded raisins
2 pounds currants
1 pound nut meats (almonds if available)
1 pound candied citron
1 pound candied orange
1 pound candied lemon
    candied cherries and candied rhubarb if desired

Cream butter, add sugar and honey and cream well. Add well beaten eggs, flour, soda and spices that have been sifted together. Add milk. Add the slightly floured fruit that has been carefully washed and dried in oven, almonds that have been blanched and dried, candied fruit cut in pieces. Mix well and place in pans that have been lined with greased brown paper. Decorate top of cake with cherries, almonds and strips of citron. Place greased paper over top of cake. Steam for 2½ hours and then bake in a slow oven (250°F.) for 2½ hours.

Honey Layer Cake

½ cup shortening
½ cup sugar
½ cup honey
2 egg yolks
2 cups sifted cake flour
3 teaspoons baking powder
¾ teaspoon salt
¾ cup milk
½ teaspoon flavoring
2 egg whites

Cream shortening thoroughly. Add sugar and honey, beat until mixture is light and fluffy. Add egg yolks and beat well. Add sifted dry ingredients alternately with milk. Add flavoring and fold in stiffly-beaten egg whites. Bake in 2 layers at 350° F. for 30 minutes.

Note: Spread Lemon, Fig, or Orange Filling between layers. If you desire a Chocolate Flake Cake, fold in with the beaten egg whites 1 cup chocolate flakes made by cutting unsweetened chocolate finely, or putting chocolate through meat grinder.

Lemon Filling

¼ cup sugar
2 tablespoons flour
¼ cup lemon juice
½ cup honey
    grated rind of 1 lemon
1 egg, slightly beaten
1 tablespoon butter

Mix ingredients in top of double boiler. Cook over hot water, stirring constantly until thickened. Cool. Spread between layers of cake.

Fig Filling

½ cup chopped figs
½ cup honey
¼ cup water
2 tablespoons orange juice
1 tablespoon corn starch

Mix ingredients in top of double boiler and cook until thick enough to spread. Spread between cake layers while hot.

Orange Filling

2 tablespoons sugar
2 tablespoons flour
½ tablespoon lemon juice
½ cup orange juice
¼ cup honey
    grated rind of 1 orange
1 egg, slightly beaten
1 tablespoon butter

Mix ingredients in top of double boiler and cook until thickened. Cool and spread between cake layers.

Loaf Cake

⅔ cup shortening
1½ cups honey
3 eggs
3 cups flour
3 teaspoons baking powder
½ teaspoon salt
1 teaspoon cinnamon
1 teaspoon mace
½ cup fruit juice
1 cup seeded raisins
1 cup chopped nuts

Cream shortening, add honey gradually. Blend well. Add well-beaten eggs. Sift dry ingredients together. Add alternately with the fruit juice. Stir in raisins and nuts. Pour into 2 loaf pans lined with well-greased waxed paper. Bake 1 hour in moderate oven (350° F.).

Applesauce Cake

⅓ cup shortening
¾ cup honey
2 cups flour
¼ teaspoon cloves
½ teaspoon cinnamon
½ teaspoon nutmeg
¼ teaspoon salt
1 teaspoon soda
1 cup cold, unsweetened applesauce
1 cup seedless raisins

Cream shortening. Add honey gradually, creaming after each addition. Mix and sift together dry ingredients and add alternately with the applesauce to the creamed mixture. Fold in raisins. Pour batter into a well-greased 8 x 8-inch pan. Bake in a moderate oven (350° F.) for about 45 minutes.

Everyday Cake

⅓ cup shortening
½ cup sugar
½ cup honey
1 egg
½ cup milk
2 cups sifted cake flour
2 teaspoons baking powder
¼ teaspoon salt
1 teaspoon lemon extract

Cream shortening. Add sugar and cream well. Add honey and beat until light and fluffy. Add egg and beat thoroughly. Add sifted dry ingredients alternately with milk. Add extract. Bake in two layers in moderate oven (375° F.) 25 to 30 minutes. Put layers together with French Honey-Chocolate Frosting.

Honey Sour Cream Spice Cup Cakes

½ cup shortening
1 cup brown sugar
1 cup honey
3 egg yolks
2 cups flour
¼ teaspoon salt
1 teaspoon ground cloves
1 teaspoon allspice
1 teaspoon cinnamon
1 teaspoon soda
1 cup thick sour cream
3 egg whites

Cream shortening. Add sugar and honey and cream well again. Add egg yolks, one at a time, and beat well. Sift dry ingredients and add alternately with the sour cream, beating after each addition. Fold in stiffly-beaten whites of eggs. Bake in greased muffin pans in a moderate oven (350° F.) 30 minutes, or in a greased cake pan for 40 minutes.

Note: If brown sugar becomes hard, put it in the bread box over night.

Nut Cake

½ cup shortening
1 cup sugar
½ cup honey
¾ cup cold water
2 cups sifted cake flour
1 cup broken nut meats
4 egg whites
4 teaspoons baking powder
1 teaspoon lemon extract

Cream shortening and sugar. Add honey. Beat well. Add flour and cold water alternately. Add half the beaten egg whites. Add the nut meats floured slightly. Fold in remainder of beaten eggs, baking powder and extract. Bake in 9 x 12-inch cake pan (350° F.) 50 to 60 minutes. Frost with uncooked Honey Frosting.

Gold Cake

¼ cup butter or margarine
½ cup honey
1 teaspoon orange extract
1 cup sifted flour
1½ teaspoons baking powder
½ teaspoon salt
4 egg yolks
¼ cup milk

Cream butter or margarine. Add honey gradually and beat well. Add extract. Sift together flour, baking powder, and salt. Add ¼ of the sifted dry ingredients. Add eggs and beat well. Add remaining ingredients. Bake 40–45 minutes in greased loaf pan in moderate oven (350° F.).

Honey Meringue

1 egg white
½ cup honey

Beat egg white with rotary or electric beater until it begins to froth. Then add honey, gradually beating until meringue stands high in peaks, (from 5 to 10 minutes beating). Use on puddings or cakes.

Spice Cake

½ cup shortening
¾ cup honey
2 cups sifted cake flour
2 teaspoons baking powder
½ teaspoon salt
1 teaspoon cinnamon
½ teaspoon cloves
¼ teaspoon nutmeg
2 eggs, separated
½ cup milk
½ cup broken nut meats
½ cup chopped raisins

Cream shortening, add honey and beat thoroughly. Mix and sift together flour, baking powder, salt, and spices. Add about 1 cup of sifted dry ingredients to shortening and honey mixture. Beat well. Add egg yolks and beat. Add remaining dry ingredients alternately with milk. Add nuts and raisins with last addition of flour. Stir in stiffly-beaten egg whites. Pour batter into greased tube pan. Bake in moderate oven (350° F.) 60 minutes, or until done.

Ginger Bread

2 cups sifted flour
2 teaspoons baking powder
1 teaspoon salt
½ teaspoon ginger
½ teaspoon cloves
½ teaspoon nutmeg
½ cup shortening
⅛ cup sugar
½ cup honey
2 eggs
¾ cup milk

Combine first seven ingredients and sift together three times. Cream shortening. Add sugar and honey and beat well. Add ½ cup of sifted dry ingredients and mix thoroughly. Add beaten eggs. Add remainder of dry ingredients alternately with milk. Bake in greased pan (375° F.) about 35 to 40 minutes. Cut into squares, and top with honey meringue.

Tutti Frutti Cake

1 cup cooked prunes
1¾ cups seedless raisins
½ cup sliced citron
⅛ cup sliced candied lemon peel
½ cup sliced candied orange peel
½ cup sliced candied cherries
2 teaspoons cinnamon
1 teaspoon mace
½ teaspoon cloves
½ teaspoon allspice
1 cup prune juice
½ cup orange juice
1 cup honey
1 cup shortening
1 cup sugar
4 eggs
1 cup broken walnut meats
5 cups sifted flour
1½ teaspoons salt
1¼ teaspoons soda

Remove pits from prunes and cut into small pieces. Rinse and drain raisins. Combine fruits and peels with spices, cover with fruit liquids and honey, blend well, and let stand over night. Cream shortening with sugar, add well-beaten eggs, and combine with fruit mixture and nuts. Add flour sifted with salt and soda, and blend thoroughly. Pour into greased paper-lined tube pan (about 10 x 4-inches). Bake in slow oven (300° F.) 3 to 3¼ hours. Before removing from oven, test with cake tester. Makes about 5 lbs. baked.

Cakes 17

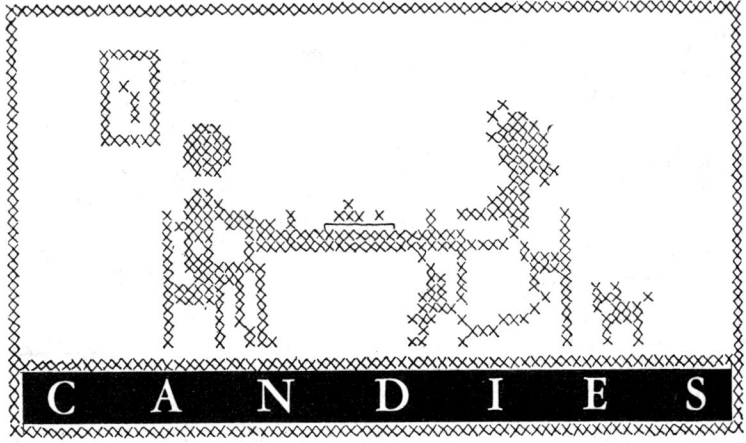

CANDIES

*"All candy calls for flavor sweet
And honey therein can't be beat."*

If the essential rules are mastered, homemade candy can equal candy made by professionals, in flavor, consistency, and appearance.

The essential rules are:
1. Use a candy thermometer as the cold water test is not accurate enough.
2. Creamy candies should not be stirred until sugar is dissolved.
3. Use cooking utensils that are smooth on the inside.
4. Creamy candies, like fudge, should be cooled before beating.
5. Taffies and brittles should be stirred only enough to prevent burning.
6. Sugar crystals which form on the inside of the pan can be brushed down with a fork wrapped in cheesecloth and dipped in cold water.
7. As soon as caramels have cooled, wrap in waxed paper.
8. Penuchi and fudge should be stored in tightly covered containers.

Candy sirup is cooked to one of five stages, depending upon the kind of candy being made:

Soft Ball	236° to 240° F.
Firm Ball	242° to 248° F.
Hard Ball	250° to 265° F.
Brittle	270° to 290° F.
Very Brittle	295° to 310° F.

Honey Fudge

2 cups sugar
1 square unsweetened chocolate
¼ teaspoon salt
1 cup evaporated milk
¼ cup honey
2 tablespoons butter
1 cup nuts

Boil sugar, chocolate, salt, and milk for five minutes. Add honey and cook to soft-ball stage (240° F.). Add butter; let stand until lukewarm; beat until creamy, add nuts, and pour into buttered pan. Cut when firm.

Honey Fondant

⅔ cup honey
4 cups sugar
2 cups boiling water

Cook honey, sugar, and water slowly. Do not let boil until sugar is dissolved. Keep crystals off side of the pan with cloth wet in cold water and wrapped around a fork. When sugar is dissolved, bring to a boil and boil slowly to the soft-ball stage (238° F.). Keeping a cover on the pan part of the time helps to keep the crystals from forming. Remove from fire and pour at once on large buttered platters. When lukewarm stir until creamy. Knead until smooth. Fondant improves if allowed to stand a few days before using. Flavor as desired.

Honey Caramels

2 cups sugar
2 cups honey
few grains of salt
½ cup butter
1 cup evaporated milk

Cook sugar, honey, and salt rapidly to hard-ball stage (250° F.). Stir occasionally. Add butter and milk gradually so the mixture does not stop boiling at any time. Cook rapidly to hard-ball stage (250° F.). Stir constantly so mixture will not stick. Pour into buttered pan and cool thoroughly before cutting into squares. Wrap individually in oiled paper.

Honey Divinity

2 cups sugar
⅓ cup honey
⅓ cup water
2 egg whites
½ cup chopped nut meats

Boil sugar, honey, and water until sirup spins a thread (278° F.). Pour sirup over well-beaten egg whites, beating continuously. Just before mixture starts to set, add chopped nut meats. When mixture crystallizes, drop with a spoon on waxed paper.

Variation: Candied cherries or candied rhubarb may be added.

Honey Taffy

2 cups sugar
2 cups honey
⅔ cup cold water
⅛ teaspoon salt

Boil sugar, honey, and water to brittle stage (288° F.). Add salt. Put in buttered dish to cool; pull until white.

Honey Bittersweets

Comb honey
hot water
confectioners' chocolate

Let comb honey remain in refrigerator 24 hours before using. Cut comb honey into pieces about ¾ inch long and ⅜ inch wide with knife that is dipped in boiling water. Place pieces on trays covered with waxed paper; chill 30 minutes. Coat with dipping chocolate. Drop a nut on each piece. (It requires a little practice to be able to turn out honeyed bittersweets that do not develop honey leaks.) It is necessary to have dipping chocolate at proper temperature (about 70 to 75° F.) when coating. Coating in a room of 60 to 65° F. will cause the chocolate to harden more quickly.

Candies 19

Spiced Honey Nuts

3 cups sifted confectioners' sugar
3 teaspoons ground cinnamon
1½ teaspoons ground nutmeg
1½ teaspoons ground allspice
1 egg white, unbeaten
2 tablespoons honey
⅛ teaspoon salt
¾ pound almond, pecan, or walnut meats

Sift sugar and spices together 3 times. Spread one half of the mixture, ¼ inch thick, on baking sheet or shallow pan. Place egg white, honey, and salt in bowl, and beat until mixed but not foamy. Add nuts and stir until coated. Place nuts on sugar, one at a time, top side up, ¼ inch apart. Cover evenly with remaining sugar mixture. Set pan inside another baking sheet, or pan, and bake in very slow oven (250° F.) 1½ hours*. Remove nuts immediately and brush off excess sugar. Cool. Store in airtight glass jar. Approximate yield: 1 pound.

* A very slow oven is necessary to make nuts crisp and to prevent them from becoming too brown.

Honey Penuche

2 cups brown sugar
¼ teaspoon salt
⅔ cup white sugar
1 cup milk
¼ cup honey
3 tablespoons butter
½ cup chopped nuts

Combine all ingredients except butter and nuts, and cook over a low flame to 240° F. Stir just enough to prevent sticking. Remove from fire, add butter, and cool to lukewarm. Do not stir. Beat until candy begins to thicken. Add nuts and turn into a greased shallow pan. When firm, cut into squares.

Cream Candy

1 cup sugar
¼ cup cream
¼ cup honey
1 tablespoon butter
½ cup chopped nuts

Mix sugar, cream, and honey. Cook until the sugar is dissolved. Add butter and continue without stirring until a very soft-ball stage is reached (236° F.). Remove from fire and begin to beat at once. Beat until thick and dull in appearance. Add nuts just before turning out. Pour into greased pan. Cut with a warm knife before the mixture is cold.

Honey Popcorn Balls

¾ cup sugar
1 teaspoon salt
½ cup water
¾ cup honey
3 quarts popcorn

Cook sugar, salt, and water (stir until sugar is dissolved) to very brittle stage (300° F.). Add honey slowly, stirring until blended. Cook again until thermometer registers 240° F. (about one minute). Pour over popcorn and form into balls. Wrap in heavy waxed paper.

Fruit Candy

¼ cup dried prunes
¼ cup dried apricots
¼ cup dried figs
½ cup dates
¼ cup raisins
⅓ cup honey

Let cleaned dried prunes and apricots stand in boiling water for five minutes. Run all the fruit through a food chopper, fine knife. Add honey. With buttered hands shape into balls. Roll in chopped nuts, cocoanut, or coat with confectioners' chocolate. Nuts may be added and other dried fruits like peaches and pears used.

Honeyed Fruit Strips

Orange peel
water
salt
honey

Remove peel from 3 oranges; cut peel into strips. Cover with water to which 1 teaspoon of salt has been added. Boil 30 minutes; drain; cover with fresh water; boil until peel is tender. Drain. Add honey enough to cover, from ¾ to 1 cup. Let *simmer very slowly* until peel is clear (about 45 minutes). Lay on waxed paper and let stand 2 or 3 days before using.

Variations: Grapefruit peel and lemon peel may be similarly prepared.
Fruit strips may be rolled in cocoanut or nuts and used as a confection.
Peel may be coated with confectioners' chocolate.
Peel may be chopped and used in cookies, nut bread, muffin mixtures.

Honey Twists

½ cup honey
1 cup sugar
½ cup milk
¼ teaspoon salt
1 teaspoon vanilla extract

Combine ingredients and cook over a low heat until when tested a hard ball is formed in cold water (260° F.). Stir occasionally. Pour into a shallow greased pan. Pull until light and firm as soon as it is cool enough to handle. Twist into rope form and cut in one or two-inch lengths. Wrap in waxed paper and store in a cool place.

Honey Marshmallows

1 tablespoon gelatine
¼ cup cold water
1 cup honey
¾ to 1 pound cocoanut

Soak gelatin well in cold water. Dissolve gelatin over hot water and add to the honey which has been warmed. Beat until very light and fluffy (about 10 minutes by machine, and 20 minutes by hand). Turn out on oiled pan and let stand 24 to 48 hours. Toast cocoanut and roll to make fine. Spread cocoanut over the surface of a large pan and turn the marshmallows on it. Dip knife into cold water and cut into squares. Roll each piece in the cocoanut.

Candies 21

Nougat

¾ cup honey
1 cup sugar
¼ teaspoon salt
½ cup water
2 egg whites
1 teaspoon flavoring
¾ cup chopped nuts

Combine honey, sugar, salt, and water and cook over low heat. Stir until sugar is dissolved and mixture starts to boil. Boil without stirring to 300° F. Pour hot sirup slowly over stiffly-beaten egg whites, beating constantly. Fold in nuts and flavoring. Spread in greased square pan. Cool and cut in rectangular pieces.

Peanut Brittle

2 cups sugar
1 cup honey
1 cup water
2 cups salted peanuts
1 tablespoon butter

Put sugar, honey, water in sauce pan. Stir until sugar is dissolved. Cook to 300° F. Remove from fire. Add butter and peanuts. Stir just enough to mix thoroughly. Pour into very thin sheets on a well-greased platter. Cool. Break into pieces to serve.

Honey Squares

¼ cup honey
2 cups sugar
3 tablespoons water
¼ teaspoon salt
1 cup nut meats, broken
1 teaspoon flavoring

Cook honey, sugar, water, and salt until soft-ball test is given. Take from fire. Add nuts and flavoring. Beat until creamy. Pour on buttered pan. Cut into squares.

Super Delicious Caramels

1½ cups thin cream
2 cups sugar
¼ cup butter
1 cup honey
½ teaspoon vanilla extract
1 cup nut meats

Cook first four ingredients over low heat to 254° F., or hard-ball stage, stirring constantly toward the end of the cooking period. Add vanilla and nuts. Pour into buttered pan. Cut when cold and wrap each in oiled paper.

Candy Roll

½ pound sweet chocolate (cooking)
3 tablespoons honey
¼ teaspoon salt
3 teaspoons cold water
1 cup peanut butter
3 tablespoons honey

Melt chocolate in top of double boiler over hot water (not boiling). Add honey and salt. Stir until smooth. Add water, about one teaspoon at a time, beating well after each addition. Beat until smooth and shiny.
Pour mixture on sheet of heavy waxed paper. Spread into rectangular shape. Let stand for 10 to 15 minutes. Blend peanut butter and the 3 tablespoons honey and spread on chocolate. Roll up like jelly roll. Wrap well in waxed paper and place in refrigerator over night. Cut in slices to serve.

CONFITURES

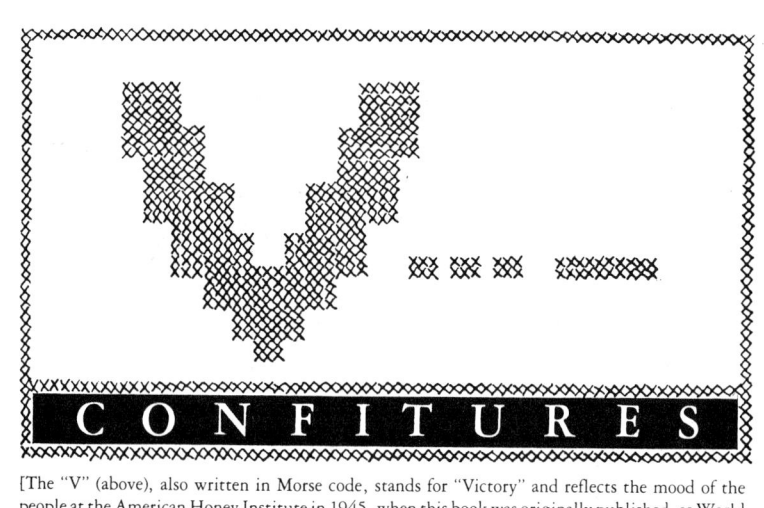

[The "V" (above), also written in Morse code, stands for "Victory" and reflects the mood of the people at the American Honey Institute in 1945, when this book was originally published, as World War II neared its end. —EDITOR]

"A little honey in the canning
Mixed with the juices is good planning."

Use a large kettle when making jelly or jams in which part or all honey is used.

Since honey contains some moisture, it is necessary to cook the mixture somewhat longer in order to obtain the desired consistency.

Currant Jelly

Pick over currants. Do not remove stems. Wash. Drain. Place in preserving kettle. Mash with potato masher. Add ½ cup water to about 2 quarts fruit. Bring to a boil, simmer until currants appear white. Strain through a jelly bag. Measure juice. Add ¾ cup honey and ¾ cup sugar to 2 cups juice. Cook only 4 cupfuls of juice at a time. Stir until sugar dissolves. Cook until two drops run together and "sheet" off spoon. Fill hot, sterilized glasses. Cover with paraffin.

Rhubarb Jelly

1 cup rhubarb juice
2 tablespoons granulated pectin
1 cup honey

Wash and cut rhubarb into inch lengths. Place in preserving kettle. Add enough water to prevent it from sticking. Cook slowly in covered kettle until soft. Strain in jelly bag. Measure juice. Add pectin and stir vigorously. Bring to a boil. Add honey and continue to boil until jelly test is secured. Fill hot, sterilized glasses with jelly. Cover with paraffin.

Sunshine Preserves

1½ cups honey
1½ cups sugar
1 quart pitted cherries

Combine honey and sugar. Bring slowly to the boiling point, add cherries and cook 12 minutes. Pour out on shallow dishes; cover with glass and allow to stand in the sunshine one day or longer. Seal in hot, sterilized glasses.

Sweet Fruit Pickles

2 cups honey
1 cup vinegar
2 inches stick cinnamon
6 whole cloves
apples

Combine honey, vinegar, and spices, and heat to boiling. Have ready 8 to 10 cups of quartered apples (pared or not, as you like). Cook 2 or 3 cups of apples at a time in the sirup, handling them gently so they will not mash. When transparent, lift out and place in a jar or bowl, and continue until all are cooked. Take out spices, pour remaining sirup over the apples, and store in sterilized jars until needed. Serve cold with meats.

Honey Chutney

2 quarts sour apples
2 green peppers
3 onions, medium
¾ pound seedless raisins
½ tablespoon salt
1 cup honey
Juice of 2 lemons and the grated rind of 1
1½ cups vinegar
¾ cup tart fruit juice
¾ tablespoon ginger
¼ teaspoon cayenne pepper

Wash and chop fruit and vegetables. Add all other ingredients and simmer until thick like Chili Sauce. Seal in hot, sterilized jars.

Honey Orange Marmalade

2 oranges, medium
¼ grapefruit, medium
⅛ lemon
4¾ cups water per pound of fruit
¾ pound sugar per pound of fruit and liquid
¼ pound honey per pound of fruit and liquid

Cut the fruit into very thin slices, cut each slice into eighths, remove the seeds, the pithy inner portion, and about ½ of the orange rind. Add the water to the fruit and let stand in the refrigerator 24 hours. Remove. Boil steadily for about 1 hour, or until the rind is tender and slightly translucent. Weigh the fruit and liquid and add the required amount of sugar. Boil slowly until it reaches 214° F., add the required amount of honey, and cook to 218° F. Remove from stove and seal in sterilized glasses. Yield: Approximately one quart.

Canned Peaches

3 cups water
½ cup sugar
½ cup honey
12 peaches

Prepare sirup by boiling water and sugar for 5 minutes. Add honey. Scald peaches in boiling water to loosen skins; peel, cut in halves and remove stones. Cook fruit in sirup. Allow 1 peach stone to 6 peaches. Cook from 5 to 10 minutes. Test by piercing with silver fork. Arrange peaches when done with cut side down in jar. Fill to overflowing with hot sirup and remove air bubbles with sterilized knife. Cover with lid just taken from boiling water. **Note: Pears may be** canned in the same way.

COOKIES

*"Of all the cookies I have eaten
Those made with honey can't be beaten."*

Everyday Cookies

½ cup shortening
½ cup sugar
½ cup honey
1 egg
⅔ cup flour
½ teaspoon soda
½ teaspoon baking powder
¼ teaspoon salt
1 cup quick cooking oats
1 cup shredded cocoanut
1 teaspoon vanilla extract
½ cup chopped nut meats

Cream shortening, sugar, and honey together until light and fluffy. Add well-beaten egg, blend together. Sift flour with dry ingredients; stir well. Add oats, cocoanut, and vanilla. Add nut meats. Spread on greased baking sheets; bake in moderate oven (350° F.). Bake about 12 to 15 minutes. Cut into bars.

Fig Newtons

1 cup honey
1 cup shortening
1 cup sugar
2 eggs
  juice and rind of ½ lemon
6½ cups flour
2 teaspoons baking powder
1 teaspoon soda
1 teaspoon salt

Cream honey, shortening, and sugar. Add beaten eggs, lemon juice, and rind. Add flour which has been sifted three times with baking powder, salt, and soda. Roll dough quite thin, cut into strips about 6 inches long and 3 inches wide. Put filling in center of the strip, and lap sides over. Bake 15 minutes, 400° F. Cool. Cut into desired size, crosswise.

Fig Filling

4 cups ground figs
1 cup honey and ¼ cup water
  juice of ½ lemon and
  ½ orange

Combine and cook 15 minutes, stirring constantly. Cool before using.

Hermits

½ cup shortening
1 cup honey
½ cup brown sugar
2 eggs, well beaten
3 tablespoons milk
2¼ cups flour
1 teaspoon baking soda
½ teaspoon cinnamon
½ teaspoon allspice
1 cup seedless raisins
1 cup currants
1 cup dates
½ cup nuts

Cream shortening, add honey and sugar, well-beaten eggs, milk and dry ingredients, fruit and nuts. Drop from teaspoon upon a greased cooky sheet. Bake at 400° F. for 10 to 12 minutes. Makes about 7¾ dozen.

Chocolate Chip Cookies

½ cup shortening
½ cup honey
1 small egg
1 cup sifted flour
1 teaspoon baking powder
¼ teaspoon salt
½ teaspoon vanilla extract
½ cup semi-sweet chocolate chips
¼ cup nut meats chopped

Cream shortening and honey until light and fluffy. Add egg and beat well. Sift flour, baking powder, and salt twice. Add flour mixture to shortening mixture; add vanilla and blend all well. Fold in chocolate chips and nuts. Chill and drop by teaspoonfuls on greased cooky sheet. Bake at 375° F. for 12 minutes.

All Honey Cookies

1 cup honey
1 cup shortening
3¾ cups flour
4⅝ teaspoons baking powder
⅙ teaspoon soda
½ teaspoon each cinnamon, cloves, and allspice

Heat honey and shortening together about 1 minute. Cool. Sift flour, baking powder, soda, and spices together. Add flour to first mixture to make a soft dough. Roll thin, cut, bake at 350° F. for 12 to 15 minutes.

Honey Pecan Cookies

½ cup shortening
1 cup honey
1 egg
¼ cup sour milk
2 cups flour
½ teaspoon soda
½ teaspoon salt
¾ cup pecans
¾ cup each of raisins, cherries, and dates

Cream shortening and honey; add the egg, sour milk, and flour which has been sifted with soda and salt. Add the nuts and fruit. Drop on greased pans and bake at 350° F. for 15 minutes.

Pecan Butterballs

1 cup butter
¼ cup honey
2 cups sifted flour
½ teaspoon salt
2 teaspoons vanilla extract
2 cups finely chopped pecans

Cream butter; add honey gradually; add flour, salt and vanilla. Mix well and add chopped nuts. Form into very small balls on a greased baking sheet and bake in a moderate oven (300° F.) for 40 to 45 minutes. Roll in powdered sugar while still hot. Cool, roll again in the powdered sugar.

Raisin Honey Gems

1½ cups honey
¾ cup shortening
1 egg, beaten
2½ cups flour
¼ teaspoon salt
¼ teaspoon soda
2¼ teaspoons baking powder
1 teaspoon cinnamon
1½ cups oatmeal (uncooked)
¾ cup raisins
2 tablespoons hot water

Cream honey and shortening. Add beaten egg. Sift flour, salt, soda, baking powder, and cinnamon into mixture. Add oatmeal, raisins, and water. Mix thoroughly. Drop by teaspoonfuls upon greased cooky sheet. Bake in moderate oven (375° F.) for 15 minutes.

Butter Cookies

1 pound butter
1 cup honey
2 eggs
grated rind of ½ lemon
8 cups flour
1¼ teaspoons baking powder
juice of ½ lemon
1 cup almonds, chopped

Cream butter, add the honey, yolks of eggs, slightly beaten; add grated rind of lemon and flour mixed with baking powder. Add lemon juice. Chill dough. The dough may be formed into small balls, rolled and cut. Brush with the white of egg and sprinkle the chopped almonds on top. Bake at 350° F. 10 to 15 minutes. (Will keep well.)

Variations

Divide dough into 8 parts. Use coloring liquid. Color one part red, another blue, one green, and one yellow. Add ½ ounce melted chocolate to one part. Keep one part natural color. Add ¼ teaspoon cinnamon, ¼ teaspoon nutmeg to one part, and any combination of fruit (dates or raisins) and chopped nuts to the last part. Many different shapes and combinations will suggest themselves; for example, roll red dough ⅛ inch thick into a rectangle, roll the green the same thickness and size. Place on top of red. Roll as for a jelly roll. Chill, cut into thin slices. Bake.

Honey Nut Brownies

¼ cup shortening
2 squares chocolate
½ cup honey
1 teaspoon vanilla extract
½ cup sugar
2 eggs
½ cup flour (sifted with ¼ teaspoon baking powder)
¼ teaspoon salt
1 cup chopped nuts

Melt shortening and chocolate together. Add honey, vanilla, sugar, and beaten eggs. Sift flour, baking powder, and salt and add nuts. Add this to first mixture. Bake in a shallow pan which has been lined with well greased waxed paper, in a slow oven (300° F.) for 45 minutes.

Honey Peanut Rocks

1 cup shortening
½ cup brown sugar
½ cup honey
2 cups flour
2½ teaspoons baking powder
1/16 teaspoon soda
⅓ cup milk
2 cups quick-cooking oatmeal
1 cup each of chopped raisins and peanuts

Cream shortening. Add brown sugar and honey gradually and cream well. Add flour sifted with baking powder and soda alternately with milk. Add the oatmeal, raisins, and peanuts. Drop from a teaspoon upon a greased cooky sheet. Bake in a slow oven (300° F.) 15 to 20 minutes.

Honey Bars

1 cup honey
3 eggs, well beaten
1 teaspoon baking powder
1⅓ cups flour
1 cup chopped nuts
1 pound chopped dates
1 teaspoon vanilla extract

Mix honey and well-beaten eggs together. Add baking powder and flour sifted together, chopped nuts, dates, and extract. Bake in a long, flat pan. Mixture should be ¼ inch deep, and ½ inch after baking. Cut into strips ½ inch wide and 3 inches long. Before serving roll in powdered sugar. These are fine for the holidays since they can be made ahead of time and will improve in flavor. (Bake at 350° F. for 15 to 20 minutes.)

Honey Gingernuts

1 cup honey
1 cup sugar
1 cup softened shortening
1 egg, beaten
2 cups flour
2 teaspoons baking powder
3 teaspoons ginger
1 cup chopped nuts
additional flour

Mix honey, sugar, shortening, and egg. Sift flour, baking powder, and ginger. Combine flour mixture with honey mixture. Add nuts. Add more flour, enough to make batter of right consistency. Drop by teaspoonfuls upon a greased cooky sheet and bake at 350° to 375° F.

Christmas Fruit Nuggets

1 cup shortening
1½ cups honey
2 eggs
3 cups sifted cake flour
3 teaspoons baking powder
¼ teaspoon salt
½ teaspoon each cloves, cinnamon, and nutmeg
½ cup milk
½ cup candied pineapple
1 cup candied cherries
1 cup candied raisins
1 cup English walnuts

Cream shortening. Add honey and cream together. Beat eggs and add. Sift together cake flour, baking powder, salt, cloves, cinnamon, nutmeg, and add alternately with milk. Chop pineapple, cherries, raisins, and walnuts. Mix all together well. Drop by teaspoonfuls either upon greased baking pan or into tiny paper cups. Bake in moderate oven (375° F.) for about 15 minutes.

Lebkuchen

4 eggs
¼ pound sugar
¼ pound honey
½ pound flour
2 teaspoons soda
3 teaspoons cinnamon
½ teaspoon cardamon
½ teaspoon cloves
⅛ pound orange peel
¼ pound citron
    grated rind of ½ lemon
¼ pound shelled almonds

Beat whole eggs until very light, add sugar and honey and sifted dry ingredients. Beat well. Add fruits and nuts. Bake in moderate oven (350° F.) in two 10 x 16-inch pans. Ice with powdered sugar and cream.

Christmas Cookies

2 cups brown sugar
½ cup honey
¼ cup shortening
1 egg
2½ cups flour
3 teaspoons baking powder
1 teaspoon cinnamon
2 ounces of citron, ground very fine
    juice of ½ orange and grated rind and juice of ½ lemon
½ cup almonds, blanched and chopped

Cook sugar and honey until sugar is dissolved. Add shortening and cool. Add beaten egg. Sift the dry ingredients and add to the sirup. Add chopped fruit, fruit juices, and nuts. If necessary, add just a bit more flour to handle it easily. Roll ⅛ inch thick and cut into fancy shapes. Bake on greased cooky sheet at 350° F. for 10 minutes.

Cookies 29

Honey Nut Cookies

2 egg whites
½ cup honey
½ cup sugar
¼ teaspoon salt
¼ cup water
1 tablespoon flavoring
1 cup chopped black walnuts

Beat egg whites with rotary beater until stiff. Gradually add honey, beating after each addition. Continue beating until mixture is stiff. Combine sugar, salt, and water in small saucepan. Cook until sugar is dissolved and mixture boils, stirring constantly. Cover tightly and boil 2 minutes. Uncover and boil, without stirring, until a small amount of sirup forms a firm ball in cold water (250° F.). Pour sirup in fine stream over egg mixture, beating constantly. Beat until cool and thickened. Add flavoring and nuts. Drop from teaspoon upon well-buttered, floured baking sheet. Bake in slow oven (300° F.) 25 to 30 minutes, or until delicately browned. Carefully remove from sheet with sharp edge of clean knife. Store in tightly covered jar with waxed paper between each layer. Approximate yield: 5 dozen cookies.

Honey Oatmeal Cookies

½ cup shortening
1 cup honey
1 egg
1½ cups sifted flour
½ teaspoon soda
½ teaspoon salt
1⅔ cups oatmeal
4 tablespoons sour milk
½ cup chopped peanuts
1 cup raisins

Cream shortening. Add the honey and blend. Stir in the egg. Sift together dry ingredients and add oatmeal. Add dry ingredients alternately with milk to shortening and honey mixture. Stir in nuts and raisins. Drop by spoonful upon a greased pan or baking sheet. Bake in a moderate oven (350° F.) for 15 minutes. Yield: 3 dozen cookies.

Honey Peanut Butter Cookies

½ cup shortening
½ cup honey
½ cup brown sugar
1 egg
½ cup peanut butter
½ teaspoon salt
1¼ cups flour
½ teaspoon soda

Cream shortening, honey, and sugar together until light and fluffy. Add well-beaten egg. Add peanut butter and salt. Stir in flour and soda sifted together and mix well. Form into small balls of dough. Place upon greased cooky sheet. Press with a fork. Bake in moderate oven (350° F.) 12 to 15 minutes.

Christmas Honey-Ginger Cookies

2 cups sifted flour
⅛ teaspoon soda
⅓ cup honey
½ teaspoon ground ginger
½ teaspoon salt
½ cup sugar
2 tablespoons water
1 egg, slightly beaten
1 teaspoon orange extract
½ cup chopped crystallized ginger
½ cup chopped blanched almonds

Sift flour once, measure, add soda and sift again. Place honey, ground ginger, salt, sugar, water, egg, and orange extract in bowl, and beat with rotary beater until well blended. Add crystallized ginger and nuts, mixing thoroughly. Stir in flour. Chill thoroughly. Place on lightly-floured board, roll ¼ inch thick, and cut into fancy Christmas shapes. Brush cookies with egg, and sprinkle with colored sugar or tiny Christmas candy mixtures. Bake on ungreased baking sheet in moderately slow oven (325° F.) 12 to 15 minutes. Cool. Store in airtight container. Approximate yield: 5 dozen (2½-inch) cookies.

Peanut Butter Brownies

¼ cup shortening
2 tablespoons peanut butter
3 tablespoons cocoa
½ cup sugar
1 egg
½ cup honey
¾ cup sifted flour
½ teaspoon baking powder
¼ teaspoon salt
½ cup nut meats

Cream shortening and peanut butter together. Add cocoa and sugar (sifted together) a little at a time. Cream well. Add egg and beat well. Add honey a little at a time and beat until well blended. Add baking powder, salt, and flour sifted together. Add nut meats. Mix well. Spread mixture in well-greased 8 x 8-inch pan. Bake in moderate oven (350° F.) for 35 minutes. Cut into 1 or 2-inch squares for serving.

Date Peanut Butter Drops

½ cup shortening
¾ cup peanut butter
½ cup sugar
½ cup honey
1 teaspoon vanilla extract
2 eggs
1 cup chopped dates
2 cups sifted enriched flour
2½ teaspoons baking powder
½ teaspoon salt
¼ cup milk

Cream together shortening, peanut butter, and sugar. Add honey and beat. Blend in vanilla extract. Beat eggs and add. Add dates. Sift together flour, baking powder, and salt, and add to creamed mixture alternately with milk. Blend well. Drop by teaspoonfuls on greased baking sheet and bake in moderate oven (350° F.) 15 minutes. Yield: 4 dozen 2-inch cookies.

Honey Jam Bars

½ cup shortening
½ cup honey
1½ cups sifted flour
1 teaspoon baking powder
½ teaspoon salt
1 teaspoon cinnamon
¼ teaspoon nutmeg
¼ teaspoon allspice
1 egg, beaten
¾ cup jam

Cream shortening. Add honey. Blend well. Add sifted dry ingredients and mix. Add beaten egg. Spread half batter in greased pan and spread with jam. Cover jam with rest of batter. Bake in hot oven (400° F.) 30 to 35 minutes. Cut into 1 x 4-inch bars. Yield: 2 dozen bars.

Eggless Honey Cookies

½ cup honey
½ cup shortening
2 cups flour
½ teaspoon cinnamon
½ teaspoon cloves
1 teaspoon soda

Heat honey and shortening carefully for a minute or two. When cool add dry ingredients that have been sifted together several times. Roll out to ¼ inch in thickness and cut with a doughnut cutter. Bake on greased cooky sheet for 12 to 15 minutes in a moderate oven (350° F.). When cold frost with a powdered sugar frosting. Decorate with clusters of red cinnamon candies and bits of green gum drops to form holly wreath design.

Chocolate Fruit Cookies

- ½ cup honey
- ½ cup sugar
- ½ cup melted shortening
- 2 eggs
- 3 squares chocolate, melted
- 1 teaspoon soda
- ½ cup milk
- 2 cups flour
- 1 cup raisins and nuts (dates may be used)
- 1 teaspoon vanilla extract

Add honey and sugar to melted shortening. Add the yolks of eggs and beat well. Add melted chocolate. Add soda to milk and then add milk and ½ the flour alternately. Mix well. Add raisins and nuts with remainder of flour. Add beaten whites of eggs and extract. Drop from teaspoon on buttered baking sheet. Bake 10 to 15 minutes at 350° F.

Honey Peanut Cookies

- 1 cup shortening
- ½ cup honey
- ½ cup brown sugar
- ⅛ cup milk
- 2 cups flour
- 1 teaspoon soda
- 1 teaspoon baking powder
- 2 cups quick-cooking oats
- 1 cup raisins, chopped
- 1 cup peanuts, chopped

Cream the shortening, add the honey, brown sugar, and the rest of the ingredients in the order given. Roll a teaspoonful of the dough in the hands, place on an ungreased cooky sheet, flattening a little. Bake in a slow oven (325° F.) for 15 to 20 minutes. Yield: 4 to 5 dozen cookies.

Chocolate Pecan Squares

- ⅔ cup flour
- ½ teaspoon baking powder
- ½ teaspoon salt
- ⅛ cup shortening
- 2 squares chocolate
- ½ cup sugar
- 2 eggs, well beaten
- ½ cup honey
- ½ cup broken pecan meats
- 1 teaspoon vanilla extract

Sift flour, baking powder, and salt together. Melt shortening and chocolate together over boiling water. Add sugar to eggs and beat well. Add honey gradually and beat thoroughly. Add shortening and chocolate mixture and beat well. Add dry ingredients, nuts, and vanilla. Place whole pecans on batter in pan before baking. Bake in greased 8 x 8 x 2-inch pans in moderate oven (350° F.) about 40 minutes. When done, cut into squares so that a pecan meat will be in center of each square.

Honey Cakes

- 3 pounds honey
- 1½ pounds sugar
- 2½ pounds flour
- ½ pound citron
- 1 tablespoon cinnamon
- 1 tablespoon cloves
- 1 teaspoon cardamon
- 1 nutmeg, grated
- 7 eggs
- 1 pound flour
- 1¼ pounds almonds
- 2 lemons, juice and rind
- 1 teaspoon baking powder (optional)

Heat honey and sugar together over low heat until sugar is dissolved. Add the flour. Remove from heat. Add the citron, cut very fine, and spices. Add beaten eggs and the one pound of flour. Add almonds, which have been ground and roasted in the oven with a little sugar until light brown. Add lemon juice and rind. Mix well. Chill dough for several days before baking. Roll dough ¼ inch thick and cut with Christmas cooky cutters. ake at 350° F. 12–15 minutes. Ice with a thin icing. Use rosewater for flavoring. The cookies should be made a month before using. Cookies keep well in a stone crock.

DESSERTS

*"If you a happy cook would be,
Use honey in your recipe."*

Honeyed Apples and Cranberries

6 medium-sized apples
½ lb. (2¼ cups) cranberries
1¾ cups water
½ cup honey
1½ cups sugar
¼ teaspoon salt
2 cinnamon sticks

Pare and core apples and place in flat-bottomed pan. Add cranberries and water and simmer 5 minutes, turning apples once during cooking period. Add remaining ingredients. Simmer 15 to 20 minutes longer, or until apples are tender. (Turn apples carefully during cooking so they are evenly red.) Remove apples to dish in which they are to be served, skim the cranberry sauce, and pour around apples. Cool. Cover tightly and place in refrigerator until ready to use. Approximate yield: 8–10 portions.

Honey Baked Pears

8 pear halves
¼ cup lemon juice
½ cup honey
1 teaspoon cinnamon
2 tablespoons butter

Arrange pears in shallow buttered baking dish. Pour over the lemon juice and honey. Sprinkle with cinnamon and dot with butter. Bake in moderate oven at 350° F. Serve hot with cream as dessert. Peaches prepared this way make a delicious dessert.

Broiled Grapefruit

Wash and dry the grapefruit and cut in half crosswise allowing one half to each person. With a sharp knife cut around and under the entire pulp being careful to leave all the membrane in the shell. Cut down on each side of each section loosening each section completely. Now with two fingers lift out the center core, to which will be attached the radiating membranes. This leaves the shell containing only the nicely separated fruit section. Spread the top of each half with honey and dot with butter. Place under the broiler flame or in a moderate oven until the honey begins to carmelize and the ingredients are well blended. Serve hot as dessert or a first course.

Baked Apple with Honey Filling

Wash and core the apples. Leave part of the core in the bottom of the apples to act as a plug. Fill the cavity with honey, using as much as the tartness of the apples requires. For variety, add a bit of lemon juice, or a few cinnamon candies. One may stuff the cavity with raisins and dates or other fruit combinations.

Honey Apple Crisp

4 cups sliced apples
¼ cup sugar
1 tablespoon lemon juice
½ cup honey
½ cup flour
¼ cup brown sugar
¼ teaspoon salt
¼ cup butter
¼ cup walnuts (if desired)

Spread sliced apples in a shallow baking dish, sprinkle with sugar and lemon juice and pour honey over all. In a bowl mix flour, brown sugar, and salt, and work in the butter as for biscuits, making a crumbly mixture. Spread these crumbs evenly over the apples and bake in a moderate oven (375° F.) for 30 to 40 minutes, or until apples are tender and crust crisply browned. Serve warm, with plain cream, or whipped cream topped with a dash of powdered cinnamon.

Marguerites

Place salted crackers in a baking pan. Spread crackers with honey and chopped nuts. Place in oven until slightly browned.

Ice Cream Sundae

Pour honey over ice cream, sprinkle nuts on top or garnish with a cherry. This is a delicious and nutritious dessert.

Honey Ice Cream

2 cups milk
¾ cup honey
¼ teaspoon salt
2 eggs
1 cup cream

Scald 2 cups whole milk, add honey and salt. Beat eggs. Pour scalded milk into the egg mixture and stir until well blended. Return to double boiler and cook for three or four minutes. Cool. Beat cream and fold into custard mixture. Freeze in refrigerator. Stir once or twice while freezing.

Honey Peppermint Ice Cream (Freezer)

1½ teaspoons gelatin
2 tablespoons water
½ cup milk
2½ cups coffee cream
⅓ cup honey
¾ cup crushed peppermint stick candy

Soak gelatin in cold water. Heat milk and cream and add honey; mix well. Add gelatin slowly, stirring constantly to prevent lumping. (Thoroughly chill if you wish to shorten freezing time.) Pour in freezer with crushed candy and freeze, or if bits of the candy are desired in the ice cream, add it after the mix has become semi-solid. Unsweetened chocolate (1 square) cut into very small pieces may be added. (A good proportion of salt and ice to use is 1 part of salt to 4 of ice.)

Pastry

1½ cups flour
½ teaspoon baking powder (optional)
½ teaspoon salt
½ cup lard or other shortening
about 4 tablespoons cold water

Sift dry ingredients. Cut or work in the shortening, leaving some of the shortening in pieces the size of a pea, and add enough cold water to hold ingredients together. Toss on a floured board and roll out carefully. This makes two crusts.

Apple Pie

6 medium sized apples (or 3 cups sliced apples)
1 tablespoon butter
1 cup honey
2 tablespoons lemon juice

Quarter and pare apples, remove core and slice. Line a 9-inch pie plate with pastry. Place the sliced apples on this. Dot with bits of butter and add a perforated upper crust, pushing it toward the center. Press edges together and trim. Bake in a hot oven (450° F.) for ten minutes; then about 30 minutes at 350° F., or until the crust is slightly browned and the fruit is soft. Remove from oven, add honey which has been mixed with lemon juice, carefully through the perforations in top crust. By the time the pie is ready to serve the honey will have been absorbed by the apples.

Honey Raisin Pie

1½ cups raisins
1 tablespoon grated orange rind
1 cup orange juice
4 tablespoons lemon juice
¾ cup honey
2 tablespoons butter
½ teaspoon salt
4 tablespoons cornstarch
¾ cup cold water
pastry for double crust (9-inch)

Rinse and drain raisins. Combine with orange rind and juice, lemon juice, honey, butter, salt, and cornstarch that has been moistened in the cold water, and stir until blended. Bring to a boil and cook and stir until mixture thickens (about 3 or 4 minutes). Pour into pastry-lined pie pan, cover with top crust. Bake in a moderately hot oven (425° F.) 30 to 35 minutes. Cool before serving. Serves 6 to 8.

Pumpkin Pie

2 cups stewed pumpkin
2 cups rich milk
1 cup honey
2 eggs
½ teaspoon salt
1 teaspoon cinnamon
½ teaspoon ginger

Mix ingredients in order given. Beat well. Pour into pastry-lined pie pan. Bake in moderate oven (350° F.) 1 hour.
For variation, replace water with orange juice in pastry recipe.
For a festive note, add pastry turkey or pumpkin designs. Roll pastry thin. Cut out, using cardboard or metal pattern. Bake on cooky sheet. When done, place on top of pie.

Peach Pie

Peaches
1 tablespoon quick cooking tapioca
½ cup honey

Line pie pan with pastry. Fill with sliced fresh peaches. Sprinkle with tapioca. Pour honey over peaches. Cover with strips of pastry. Bake in hot oven (425° F.) about 40 minutes.

Desserts

Pecan Pie

½ cup honey
½ cup brown sugar
¼ cup butter
3 eggs, beaten
1 cup pecan meats

Blend honey and sugar together. Cook slowly to form a smooth sirup. Add butter. Add beaten eggs and broken pecan meats. Pour into pie pan lined with pastry. Bake in moderate oven (400° F.) 10 minutes. Reduce temperature to 350° F. and bake for 30 minutes, or until mixture sets.

Chiffon Pie

1 tablespoon gelatin
¼ cup cold water
3 egg yolks
½ cup honey
¼ cup orange juice
3 tablespoons lemon juice
3 egg whites

Soak gelatin in cold water. Place egg yolks and honey in top of double boiler. Stir well. Add orange and lemon juices. Cook slowly over hot water stirring constantly until thickened. Add gelatin and stir until dissolved. Remove from heat. Chill. When mixture begins to settle, fold in the stiffly-beaten egg whites. Pour into baked pastry shell. Chill.

Deep-Dish Apple Pie

Wash and quarter apples. Pare. Cut into thin slices. Fill deep pie plate with apple slices. Pour 1 cup honey to which 1 tablespoon lemon juice has been added over apples. Sprinkle with cinnamon. Dot with butter. Cover with pastry. Prick design in crust to allow steam to escape and for decoration. Bake in moderately hot oven (400° F.) about 40 minutes.

Berry Pie

3 cups berries
¾ to 1 cup honey
2 tablespoons cornstarch or 4 tablespoons flour
½ teaspoon cinnamon
1 tablespoon butter

Pick over and wash berries. Place in pastry-lined pie pan. Add a little honey to cornstarch. Blend well. Add remainder of honey. Pour over berries. Add a dash of cinnamon and dot with bits of butter. Cover with criss-cross pastry. Bake in hot oven (450° F.) 10 minutes. Reduce heat to 350° F. and bake 30 minutes.

Pumpkin Chiffon Pie

¼ cup cold water
1¼ cups pumpkin
½ cup honey
3 eggs, separated
½ cup milk
½ teaspoon ginger
1 teaspoon cinnamon
½ teaspoon nutmeg
¼ teaspoon salt
½ cup sugar

Soak gelatin in water. To the pumpkin add honey, egg yolks beaten, milk, spices, and salt. Beat well. Cook over boiling water until mixture thickens. Add softened gelatin. Stir well. Chill until partially set. Add egg whites beaten with sugar. Pour into baked pastry shell. Chill. Serve with a spoonful of Honey Meringue.

Honey Delight

1 package lemon or orange flavored gelatin
½ cup boiling water
½ cup honey
juice of ½ lemon
1 can evaporated milk
½ pound vanilla wafers

Dissolve gelatin in boiling water. Add honey and lemon juice and mix well. Fold in the evaporated milk that has been chilled and whipped. Pour this mixture into a pan that has been lined with crushed vanilla wafers. Place crushed vanilla wafers on top of mixture and put in refrigerator to set. Cut into squares. Serves 6.

Fruit Rice Ring

3 tablespoons cornstarch
½ teaspoon salt
2 eggs
1½ cups milk
1 tablespoon butter
¼ cup honey
2 cups cooked rice

Put cornstarch and salt in top of double boiler. Add egg yolks and milk. Stir well. Cook over boiling water, stirring constantly until mixture thickens. Remove from heat. Add butter, honey, and rice. Fold in beaten whites of eggs. Turn into buttered ring mold. Bake in moderate oven (350° F.) 30 minutes. Cool. Unmold carefully. Fill center with fruit.

Honey Custard

¼ teaspoon salt
3 eggs, slightly beaten
¼ cup honey
2 cups milk, scalded
nutmeg

Add salt to eggs. Beat eggs just long enough to combine whites and yolks. Add honey to milk. Add honey and milk mixture slowly to eggs. Pour into custard cups. Top with a few gratings of nutmeg. Set custard cups in pan of hot water. Bake in moderate oven (325° F.) about 40 minutes, or until custard is firm.

American Pudding

¾ cup sifted flour
1 teaspoon baking powder
½ teaspoon salt
4 tablespoons butter
⅓ cup sugar
½ cup milk
4 tablespoons currants
1½ teaspoons grated lemon rind
½ cup honey
1¼ cups boiling water

Sift flour once, measure, add baking powder and salt, and sift again. Cream 2 tablespoons of the butter, add sugar gradually, creaming after each addition. Add 2 tablespoons of the milk and beat thoroughly. Add flour, alternately with remaining milk, a small amount at a time, beating after each addition until smooth. Add currants and lemon rind. Turn into well-greased baking dish, 8 x 8 x 2-inches. Combine remaining butter, honey, water, and dash of salt. Pour over batter. Bake in moderate oven (350° F.) 40 to 45 minutes. Serve warm with cream. Approximate yield: 6 portions.

Honey Hard Sauce

Cream ⅓ cup butter and beat in gradually ¾ cup honey. Add 1 teaspoon lemon juice. Chill.

Honey Steamed Pudding

¼ cup butter
½ cup honey
1 egg, well beaten
2¼ cups sifted flour
3½ teaspoons baking powder
¼ teaspoon salt
1 cup milk
½ teaspoon vanilla extract

Cream butter, add honey gradually and then the well beaten egg. Add the sifted dry ingredients and milk alternately. Add vanilla. Fill buttered individual molds ¾ full. Cover loosely with wax paper held in place with a rubber band. Place molds in a steamer for 30 minutes. Test with a toothpick. Serve hot. (Makes 12 molds).

Pudding Sauce

¼ cup sugar
6 tablespoons flour
½ cup honey
2 cups water
⅛ cup butter
juice of 1 lemon and 1 orange

Mix sugar and flour, add honey and water. Cook in double boiler until thickened. Add butter and fruit juice. Serve hot.

Rice Pudding

2 cups cooked rice
3 cups milk
¾ cup honey
3 eggs
1 cup chopped raisins

Mix rice, milk and honey. Add the eggs which have been slightly beaten. Stir in the chopped raisins. Bake at about 350° F. in a well-greased baking dish for about one hour. Serve with cream if desired. Serves 8.

Cranberry Pudding

2 cups large cranberries, cut in two and mixed with 1½ cups flour
⅔ cup honey
⅛ cup hot water
1 teaspoon soda
½ teaspoon salt
½ teaspoon baking powder

Add dry ingredients to the cranberries mixed with the flour. Mix honey and hot water and add. Put in steamer and steam two hours. Serve with the following honey sauce.

Honey Sauce

½ cup butter
⅔ cup honey
2 tablespoons flour
2 eggs, slightly beaten
½ cup lemon juice
½ pint whipped cream

Mix and cook first four ingredients slowly in double boiler until thickened. Remove from fire. Add lemon juice. When cool and ready to serve, fold in whipped cream.

French Apple Dumpling

2 cups flour
4 teaspoons baking powder
½ teaspoon salt
¼ cup lard
¾ cup milk
4 large apples
½ cup sugar
¼ teaspoon cinnamon
   melted butter

Mix ingredients as for biscuit dough. Handle as lightly as possible. Roll out the dough on a floured towel one-fourth inch thick. Cover the dough with the sliced apples, and sprinkle over the apples the one-half cup sugar and the cinnamon. Roll like a jelly roll and cut into one-inch slices. (Makes 8 slices.) Place slices in a buttered baking pan. Put one teaspoon melted butter over each roll. Bake at 400° F, 20 to 25 minutes.

Honey Dumpling Sauce

1½ cups honey
2 tablespoons cornstarch
1½ cups water
⅛ teaspoon salt
1 tablespoon butter

Mix the ingredients and cook until clear. Add ½ teaspoon vanilla. Serve on the hot slices.

Tart Pastry

2 cups flour
½ teaspoon salt
½ cup shortening
1 cup cottage cheese
3 tablespoons honey

Sift dry ingredients and cut in shortening as for pie pastry. Add honey to the cheese. Add cheese to the flour mixture and blend with pastry cutter or knives. If cheese is not moist enough to make a good pastry, add a few drops of cold water. Roll thin on lightly-floured board.

Banbury Tarts

1 cup chopped raisins
¾ cup honey
3 tablespoons cracker crumbs
1 slightly beaten egg
1 tablespoon melted butter
⅛ teaspoon salt
½ lemon, juice and grated rind

Combine all ingredients. Roll Tart Pastry thin and cut into three-inch squares. Place a teaspoon of Banbury mixture in the center of each square; cut edges, fold like a triangle and press edges together. Prick several times to allow steam to escape. Bake in hot oven (450° F.) for 15 minutes.

Coventry Tartlets

½ pound cottage or cream cheese
½ cup honey
¼ cup butter
2 egg yolks
½ teaspoon salt
¼ teaspoon nutmeg
1 tablespoon orange juice

Combine all ingredients until of a creamy consistency. Line a dozen individual tart molds with Tart Pastry. Prick and fill with the cheese mixture. Bake in a hot oven (450° F.) for 10 minutes, reduce the heat to 325° F. and bake until golden brown and firm. Remove from the oven and cool. When ready to serve, garnish with red or green honey jelly.

Desserts 39

Rhubarb Tarts

2 cups rhubarb
2 egg yolks
¾ cup honey
3 tablespoons flour
¼ teaspoon salt
2 egg whites
2 tablespoons honey

Wash and cut rhubarb in ½-inch lengths. Pour boiling water over the rhubarb and drain in colander. Mix egg yolks slightly beaten, honey, flour, and salt. Add to rhubarb. Pour into pastry lined muffin pans. Bake in moderate oven (350° F.) 30 minutes or until done. Top with meringue made by adding 2 tablespoons honey to 2 stiffly-beaten egg whites.

Tapioca Cream

⅓ cup quick cooking tapioca
⅓ cup honey
¼ teaspoon salt
2 eggs
4 cups milk, scalded
1 teaspoon vanilla extract

Combine tapioca, honey, salt, and egg yolks in top of double boiler. Add milk slowly and mix thoroughly. Cook until tapioca is transparent, stirring often. Remove from the heat and fold into the stiffly-beaten egg whites. Add the vanilla. This may be served either warm or cold with cream.

Rhubarb Brown Betty

2 cups bread crumbs
3 cups rhubarb cut in ½-inch pieces (apples may be used)
½ cup honey
¼ cup water
½ teaspoon nutmeg
3 tablespoons butter

Mix ¾ of the bread crumbs and ¾ fruit and place in a deep baking dish. Bring honey and water to a boil. Pour over bread and fruit mixture. Sprinkle remainder of crumbs over this, sprinkle with nutmeg and dot with butter. Arrange the rest of the fruit so that each serving will have one or more pieces of fruit on top. Bake in moderate oven (315° F.) 30 to 40 minutes.

Honey Parfait

2 eggs, separated
pinch salt
½ cup honey
1 teaspoon vanilla extract
1⅔ cups evaporated milk, chilled

Beat egg whites until foamy. Add honey gradually. Beat constantly. Add egg yolks and vanilla. Beat until well blended. Fold in stiffly beaten, chilled milk. Garnish with maraschino cherries. Pour into freezing trays. Serves 8.

Rhubarb Medley

3 cups rhubarb
1 cup honey
cinnamon candies
2 eggs
1 tablespoon gelatin

Wash rhubarb and cut into pieces of about 1-inch in length. Place in sauce pan. Add 1 cup honey and enough water to prevent it from scorching. Cover and cook slowly until tender. During last five minutes add enough cinnamon candies to give it a deep pink color. Add a little of the hot mixture to 2 beaten egg yolks. Return to sauce pan. Soften 1 tablespoon of gelatin in a little cold water in large bowl. Gradually add hot mixture to this. Just before it begins to set, fold in the two egg whites that have been stiffly beaten. Pour into molds and chill. Serve with whipped cream.

MEATS

*"A drop or two of Nature's sweet
Will give a better taste to meat."*

Baked Ham

1 ham
1 cup honey
cloves

Select a good quality ham. Wipe meat with a damp cloth and remove unsightly parts. Place ham fat side up in roasting pan. Add no water. Bake uncovered in slow oven (300° F.). Insert a meat thermometer with the bulb at the center of the largest muscle. Cook until the thermometer registers an internal temperature of 170° F. 25 to 30 minutes per pound should be allowed for roasting time. Before the ham is done, take from the oven and remove the rind. Mark fat into squares. Place whole clove in each square. Pour a honey glaze over ham. Return to oven to finish baking. Baste frequently.

Honey Glazes

Chopped maraschino cherries and whole almonds mixed with 1 cup honey.
1 cup honey mixed with 1 cup apricot pulp. (For attractiveness use apricot halves in flower design with whole cloves or angelica as stems.)
Crushed pineapple with 1 cup honey.
Tart cherries and honey.
1 cup honey—½ cup orange juice.
1 cup honey—½ cup cranberry sauce.
1 cup honey—½ cup cider.
For decoration use orange slices and maraschino cherries held in place on ham with cloves.

Raisin Sauce

1 cup quartered or seedless raisins
1 cup water
¼ cup honey
1 tablespoon lemon juice

Put raisins and water in sauce pan. Simmer until raisins are softened. Add honey. Boil gently for fifteen minutes. Just before serving add lemon juice.

Sweet Horseradish Sauce

¼ cup honey
¼ cup mayonnaise
½ cup whipping cream
3 tablespoons horseradish
1 teaspoon mustard
¼ teaspoon salt
1 teaspoon vinegar

Add honey to mayonnaise. Fold in the whipped cream. Add horseradish, mustard, salt, and vinegar. Store in refrigerator until ready to use.

Honey Spiced Broiled Ham

1 slice ham, 1-inch thick
¾ cup honey
½ teaspoon cloves
½ teaspoon allspice
½ teaspoon cinnamon

Wipe meat with a damp cloth. Place meat on a broiler rack allowing three inches between the top of the meat and source of heat, if possible. Sprinkle with spices and cook until browned, basting with the honey occasionally. When brown, turn. Sprinkle other side with remaining spices and continue cooking, basting occasionally with remaining honey.

Canadian Bacon, Fruited and Honeyed

6 slices Canadian Style Bacon
1 cup water
1 cup honey
1 cup raisins
6 slices pineapple

Have bacon sliced one-half inch thick. Place in dripping pan and into an oven of 350° F. Bring water to the boiling point, add the honey, stir until well mixed; then add the raisins and simmer for 10 minutes. When the meat has been in the oven 1 hour, place a slice of pineapple over each piece of bacon, pour the honey sirup containing the raisins over the bacon and pineapple. Return to the oven for 15 minutes.

Lamb Chops with Honey-Mint Sauce

Select rib, loin or shoulder lamb chops. Set the regulator of the range for broiling. Place the chops so that there is a distance of about three inches between the top of the chops and the source of heat. If the distance must be less, reduce the temperature accordingly so that the chops will broil at a moderate temperature. When the chops are browned on one side, season, turn and finish the cooking on the second side. Frequently during broiling, baste with honey-mint sauce. Chops cut 1 inch thick require 12 to 15 minutes for broiling.

Honey-Mint Sauce

½ cup water
1 tablespoon vinegar
1 cup honey
¼ cup chopped mint

Heat the water and the vinegar. Add the honey, stir well, then add the chopped mint. Cook slowly for five minutes. This sauce can be used to baste lamb chops or lamb roast during cooking or can be served with the meat at the table.

SALADS

"If honey is used with the fruit
The flavor will your palate suit."

Fruit Salad

white grapes
1 orange
1 banana
1 pear or peach
1 small apple
1 lemon
lettuce

Cut grapes into halves and remove seeds. Cut orange into halves and remove sections with a sharp-pointed knife. Slice banana and pear, or peach, and dice the apple. Pour juice of lemon over apple and banana. Moisten all fruit with honey and serve on crisp lettuce or chicory.

Pear Salad

Pears
Pimento cheese
Honey French Dressing
Lettuce

If canned pears are used, place can in refrigerator to chill pears before making up salad. Allow ½ pear to a person. Place cut side down on lettuce. Cover pear with riced pimento cheese and serve with Honey French Dressing. Rice cheese the same way one rices potatoes.

French Salad Bowl

Place a crust of bread rubbed with garlic in large bowl while tossing the salad with Honey French Dressing. Use any one or a combination of crisp salad greens such as lettuce, romaine, watercress, endive, pepper grass, or chicory. Serve at once.

Avocado Pear Salad

Combine equal parts of honey and lemon juice. Beat well and serve over slices of avocado pear and sections of grapefruit on crisp lettuce. Garnish with berries. Suggestion: A dash of paprika or chopped parsley may be added if desired.

Fruit Salad Platter

Place a small dish filled with salad dressing in center of a large platter. Place a large cup-like lettuce leaf for each person around the bowl. In each lettuce leaf place canned pear half, fig, peach, cherries, or other fruit. Prunes stuffed with equal parts peanut butter and honey, or cream cheese and honey, may be placed between salads for garnish, or a cheese ball made by adding enough honey to cream cheese to soften. Make into ball shape and roll in finely chopped nut meats or finely chopped parsley.

Stuffed Tomato Salad

Select even-sized, firm red tomatoes. Wash, scald in boiling water to loosen skin. Remove skin. Hollow the tomatoes. Sprinkle inside with salt. Drain. Chill. Fill and pile high with (1) chicken or fish salad, (2) cole slaw, (3) cottage cheese and chives. Top with a spoonful of Honey Mayonnaise and stuffed olive.

Fruit Salad Dressing

½ cup lemon juice or other fruit juice
2 teaspoons flour
⅛ teaspoon salt
¼ cup honey
2 eggs yolks
1 cup whipped cream

Blend lemon juice, flour, salt, and honey until smooth. Cook in the top of double boiler until thickened. Beat yolks of eggs and gradually add the lemon mixture. When well blended return to double boiler and cook about 2 minutes until custard-like in texture. Remove from fire and chill. When ready to use, combine with 1 cup of whipped cream.

Lemon Cream Salad Dressing

3 tablespoons honey
1 tablespoon lemon juice
1 cup whipped cream

Combine honey and lemon juice. Add to whipped cream. Serve on fruit salad.

French Dressing

½ cup salad oil
½ cup lemon juice
½ cup honey
½ teaspoon paprika
½ teaspoon salt

Place all in a tightly-covered quart jar and shake vigorously just before using.

Roquefort Cheese Dressing

Crumble with a fork ¼ pound of Roquefort cheese into small pieces. Add to 1 cup of French Dressing.

Thousand Island Dressing

To one cup Mayonnaise Dressing add finely minced stuffed olives, small onion, a little green pepper, and ½ cup chili sauce. Fold in ½ cup whipped cream.

Frozen Fruit Salad

4 ounces cream cheese
3 tablespoons mayonnaise
2 tablespoons honey
1 cup pitted white cherries
3 slices of pineapple
½ pint whipping cream

Mix cream cheese with mayonnaise, add honey and mix well. Add cherries and pineapple and fold in whipped cream. Place in freezing tray.

Honey French Dressing

½ cup honey
1 cup salad oil
½ teaspoon salt
⅛ cup chili sauce
½ cup vinegar
1 medium onion grated
1 tablespoon Worcestershire sauce

Place all ingredients in a quart jar and shake well. Serve this dressing on the lettuce and place a portion of the frozen salad on top. This dressing may be used on other salads.

Boiled Dressing

1 teaspoon mustard
1 teaspoon salt
⅛ teaspoon cayenne
2 tablespoons flour
1 cup milk
3 tablespoons honey
2 egg yolks
½ cup vinegar
1 tablespoon butter

Mix dry ingredients in top of double boiler, add milk, honey, and egg yolks. Stir well. Cook over hot water until thickened. Add vinegar and butter. Mix well until smooth mixture is formed.

Salad Dressing for Fruit

1 egg
1 tablespoon cornstarch
  pinch salt
2 tablespoons honey
1 cup pineapple juice
2 tablespoons lemon juice

Put slightly beaten egg, cornstarch, salt, and honey in top of double boiler. Add juices. Cook slowly over hot water until mixture thickens.

Cole Slaw

4 cups finely shredded cabbage

Beat 1 cup sour cream (cold) until thick. Add ¼ cup vinegar, ¼ cup honey, 1 teaspoon salt, and 2 teaspoons celery salt.

Salads 45

SANDWICHES

*"Let honey add that flavor rare
To sandwiches that you prepare."*

Honey Butter

½ cup butter
½ to 1 cup honey

Cream butter well. Add honey gradually. Beat thoroughly. Place in refrigerator. Delicious on toast, hot breads, waffles, and for sandwich filling.

Rolled Sandwich

Spread creamed honey butter on cut end of bread loaf. Cut slice of bread thin and remove crust. Sprinkle chopped nuts on honey butter. Roll slice and fasten with toothpick. Seal open edge with honey butter. Cover with waxed paper. Place in refrigerator to chill.

Tea Sandwich

With a biscuit cutter cut circles from bread slices. Spread circles of bread with softened butter and top with cream cheese softened with honey. On this spread red raspberry jam. Place a dot of cream cheese mixture or whipped cream in the center.

Toasted Tea Sandwich

Use circles cut from bread as in above recipe. Toast until brown on both sides. Spread with honey butter. Sprinkle with chopped nuts. Place under broiler until nuts are slightly browned and serve while hot.

Cream Cheese Sandwich Filling

Soften cream cheese with enough honey to spread well. Add chopped raisins or nuts.

Fruit Filling

¼ cup each dried p r u n e s, dates, figs, orange peel
1 tablespoon candied ginger
¼ cup honey

Chop fruit and blend with honey. Use between slices of buttered bread.

VEGETABLES

*"Here honey lends refining touch
If not too spare or not too much."*

Baked Squash

Wash squash and cut in half lengthwise. Remove seeds. To each half add 1 tablespoon of honey and one or two little pork sausage links. Bake at 400° F. until squash is tender and sausages brown.

Glazed Onions or Carrots

Cook small white onions or carrots in boiling salted water about 20 to 30 minutes, or until tender. Drain. Let stand a few minutes to dry. Melt four tablespoons butter in pan. Add ¼ cup honey. When well blended, add onions or carrots and cook slowly until browned and well glazed. Turn vegetables occasionally for an even glaze.

Candied Sweet Potatoes

Boil 6 medium-sized sweet potatoes without paring them. When tender drain and remove the skins. Cut in half lengthwise and arrange in a buttered baking dish. Season with salt. Heat ¼ cup butter, ½ cup honey, ½ cup orange juice, add to potatoes. Bake in quick oven (400° F.) until potatoes are brown.

Sweet-Sour Cabbage

4 cups shredded cabbage
½ cup diced bacon
3 tablespoons flour
¼ cup honey
¼ cup vinegar
½ cup water
1 teaspoon onion, chopped

Cook shredded cabbage in boiling salted water until tender. Drain. Dice bacon. Cook until well done. Remove bacon and place on cabbage. Blend bacon fat with flour. Add honey, vinegar, water, and chopped onion. Cook until thickened. Pour over cabbage and bacon. Season to taste. Heat thoroughly. Serve hot.

Note: This same recipe may be used with cooked potatoes instead of cabbage.

Sweet Potato Orange Casserole

6 cooked and sliced sweet potatoes
¼ cup butter
2 small oranges
½ cup honey
½ cup orange juice
¼ cup bread crumbs

Place a layer of sliced sweet potatoes in a greased baking dish. Dot with butter and place a layer of sliced orange (not peeled) on top. Repeat this arrangement of sweet potatoes and orange slices. Mix honey with orange juice and pour over all. Cover with buttered bread crumbs. Cover and bake about 30 minutes at 375° F. Remove cover last 10 minutes to brown crumbs.

Family Beets

Slice cooked beets. Keep warm. Cover with the following sauce:

1 tablespoon cornstarch
½ cup vinegar
a few whole cloves
¾ cup honey
1 tablespoon butter

Add cornstarch, vinegar, and a few whole cloves (mixed together) to honey. Bring to a slow boil and boil 5 minutes. Add butter. Pour over beets and let stand 20 minutes. Serve hot.

Scalloped Tomatoes

2 cups cooked tomatoes
½ teaspoon salt
pepper
2 tablespoons butter
2 tablespoons honey
1 cup cracker crumbs

Cover bottom of buttered baking dish with a layer of tomatoes. On this sprinkle salt, pepper, dots of butter and honey. Cover with a layer of cracker crumbs. Repeat with another layer of tomatoes, crumbs, and seasoning. Bake 20 minutes in a hot oven.

Baked Beans

Soak 2 cups washed beans in 4 cups of cold water over night. In the morning drain off any water that has not been absorbed. Cover the beans with fresh cold water and cook over a low flame in a tightly-covered saucepan. Do not allow the beans to boil. Let them simmer for 1¼ hours. Again drain the beans, saving the water. Prepare the bean pot by placing about ½ pound of scored salt pork in the bottom. Add the beans, cover with the following mixture: use the bean water that has been drained from the beans, and add to it ½ cup of honey; if no bean water was left over, use plain boiling water. Mix 1 teaspoon salt, 1 teaspoon dry mustard, 1 teaspoon ginger, if desired, and 1 tablespoon of finely-chopped onion with a little of the honey water. Add remainder of the honey bean water to this seasoning and pour over the beans. Place small pieces of salt pork on top. (Bacon may be used.) Cover bean pot and bake in a slow oven about 6 hours. Uncover the bean pot during the last hour of baking. If the beans become too dry, it may be necessary to add a little water.

PART TWO

New Favorite Honey Recipes

Appetizers

Holiday Entertaining

Honey Nog Punch Bowl*
Cheese Bowl* — Crackers, Potato Chips, Icebox Rye
Deviled Ham Ribbon Sandwiches   Spice Cake*

All Year Fresh Fruit Cup

2½ cups orange sections	
1 cup banana slices	
1 cup unpeeled, red-skinned apple slices	
1 cup orange juice	
Dash of lemon juice	
Honey to taste	
Berries or cherries for garnish	

Combine and serve chilled as appetizer or dessert. Yield: 6 servings.

Melon Ball Cocktail

Cantaloupe
Watermelon
Honeydew melon
Honey
Lemon juice

Cut balls from melons with a ball cutter or use a half-teaspoon size measuring spoon.

Arrange in sherbet glasses. Pour equal parts of honey and lemon juice over fruit. Garnish with berries in season or with little candy "licorice men."

---

*Recipe appears in New Favorite Honey Recipes.

Pineapple Winter Cocktail

1 package frozen fresh pineapple
2 large grapefruit
1 medium-size avocado

Partially thaw the frozen pineapple. It should still be slightly frosty. Drain. Pare the grapefruit with a sharp knife, cutting off all the outer membrane. Then slip out the sections from between the membrane walls. Peel and dice the avocado. Combine the fruits, heap lightly in sherbet glasses and cover with this dressing:

¼ cup sirup from the pineapple
¼ cup lemon juice
¼ cup honey

Garnish with sprigs of mint, water cress, sliced raw cranberries, or cubes of bright jelly. Yield: 6 to 8 servings.

Cheese Bowl

½ pound cream cheese
⅛ to ¼ pound Roquefort cheese
½ pound pimento cheese
2 tablespoons butter
2 tablespoons honey
½ teaspoon Worcestershire Sauce
Dash of cayenne

Melt cheese in upper part of double boiler, stirring constantly. Add butter, honey, Worcestershire Sauce and cayenne. Beat until fluffy. Add salt if desired. Thin, if necessary, with cooked salad dressing or mayonnaise. To serve, set bowl of this cheese whip in center of large round plate with crisp potato chips, crackers or icebox rye bordering bowl.

Beverages

Bridge Dessert

All Honey Chocolate Cake*

Coffee

Honeyed Fruit Punch

1	cup orange juice
½	cup lemon juice
2	cups grape juice
2	cups water
4	tablespoons honey

Mix thoroughly. Chill. Serve cold. Yield: 6 servings.

Hot Chocolate

2	squares unsweetened chocolate
1	cup water
¼	cup honey
⅛	teaspoon salt
3	cups milk

Place chocolate and water in sauce pan. Cook, stirring constantly, until well blended. Add honey and salt and boil 3 minutes, stirring constantly. Add milk gradually. Place over heat until mixture is hot enough to serve. Beat with **rotary egg beater**. Yield: 6 servings.

Lemon Honeyade

1 lemon
1 to 3 tablespoons honey
1 cup water
Ice

Extract lemon juice. Add honey to taste. Stir to dissolve. Add water. Serve over ice in large glasses. Garnish with lemon slice on rim—add a cherry, berry or sprig of mint if desired.

Orange Honeyade

2 cups orange juice
½ cup lemon juice
½ cup honey
1 cup water

Combine ingredients and stir well to dissolve honey. Pour over cracked ice in tall glasses. Garnish with orange slices, mint sprigs and berries or cherries.

Iced Coffee

Make double strength coffee by using 4 tablespoons coffee to 1 cup water. Pour at once into glasses filled with crushed ice. Serve with honey and top with whipped cream. Dust with cinnamon and nutmeg if desired.

Iced Tea

Make fresh tea double strength. Strain and pour over crushed ice in tall glasses. Serve with equal parts of honey and lemon juice well blended. Garnish with fresh mint leaves.

Mulled Cider

2 quarts cider
1 inch stick cinnamon
¼ teaspoon nutmeg
¼ teaspoon allspice
6 whole cloves
½ cup honey

Combine cider, spices, honey. Heat slowly. Simmer 20 minutes. Serve hot in warm mugs. Add slice of orange or lemon, a maraschino cherry and a whole clove.

Spiced Tea

1 box stick cinnamon (1¼ ounces)
1 box whole cloves (1¼ ounces)
¾ cup honey
3 oranges, juice of 3 and grated rind of 1
6 lemons, juice of 6 and grated rind of 1
⅓ cup black tea
5 quarts water, boiling

Cook spices, honey and grated rind with 2 cups water for 10 minutes. Let stand 1 hour. Strain. Steep tea in the boiling water 1 minute. Then add fruit juice and spice mixture. Serve hot. Yield: 45 cups.

Party Punch

2 cups honey
1 cup hot water
1 cup lemon juice
3 cups orange juice
1 cup mint leaves
3 quarts pineapple juice (unsweetened)
3 quarts water
4 quarts ginger ale
1 cup maraschino cherries

Add honey to hot water. Mix well. Add fruit juices, mint leaves and water. Chill thoroughly. Just before serving add ginger ale and cherries. Pour over ice cubes in punch bowl. Yield: 40 servings.

Beverages

Honey Nog Punch Bowl
(For Holiday Entertaining)

1 whole egg
2 egg yolks
3 tablespoons honey
1/16 teaspoon salt
1 pint milk

Meringue:
2 egg whites
1/8 teaspoon salt, scant
2 tablespoons honey
Cinnamon, nutmeg

Beat whole egg and yolks slightly. Add honey and salt. Blend thoroughly. Add milk. Chill several hours or overnight. Just before serving prepare meringue: Add salt to egg whites and beat to a stiff foam, add honey gradually and beat until stiff. Blend or fold into eggnog, leaving the surface fluffy with meringue. Dust with cinnamon and nutmeg. Yield: 12 punch cups.

Fruit Punch

1 cup berries in season
1 cup honey
1½ cups orange juice
½ cup lemon juice
2 cups double strength tea, freshly made
1 pint ginger ale

Crush berries and combine all ingredients except ginger ale. Chill. When ready to serve add ginger ale and crushed ice. Yield: 20 servings.

Breads

Sunday Dinner

Rib Roast of Beef

Brown Gravy

Baked Potatoes   Asparagus with Lemon Butter

Hot Honey Tea Biscuits*

Honey Orange Cake*   Coffee

Fruited Coffee Square

1½ cups sifted enriched flour
2 teaspoons baking powder
½ teaspoon salt
1 egg
½ cup honey
½ cup milk
3 tablespoons melted shortening

Sift together flour, baking powder, and salt. Beat egg, and add honey, milk, and shortening. Blend thoroughly. Add to flour mixture, stirring only enough to moisten flour. Pour into greased pan, 8x8x2-inches. Spread cranberry mixture over top, sprinkle with streusel and bake in moderate oven (375° F.) about 35 minutes. Yield: 16 2-inch squares; 1 coffee cake, 8x8-inches.

Cranberry Topping

1 cup ground cranberries
½ cup mincemeat
¼ cup honey

Mix well and spread over batter.

Streusel

¼ cup enriched flour
2 tablespoons margarine or butter
¼ cup honey

Mix ingredients. Sprinkle over cranberry topping mixture.

Honey Kuchen

Topping:
- ¼ cup brown sugar
- ½ teaspoon cinnamon
- ¼ teaspoon nutmeg
- 2 tablespoons melted butter or margarine
- ½ cup wheat flakes or bran flakes

Mix together brown sugar, spices, melted butter, and flakes. Set aside for use on top of batter.

Kuchen:
- ¾ cup sifted flour
- 2½ teaspoons baking powder
- ¼ teaspoon salt
- ½ cup milk
- ¼ cup honey
- 1 egg
- 3 tablespoons melted fat
- 1½ cups wheat flakes or bran flakes

To sifted flour add baking powder and salt, and resift. Combine milk, honey and well-beaten egg, and add to flour mixture. Add fat, mixing only enough to combine. Fold in flakes. Pour into greased pan. Sprinkle topping over batter. Bake in moderately hot oven (400° F.) 25 minutes, or until done. Yield: 1 square (8x8x2-inch pan).

Hot Cross Buns

- 2 packages yeast, compressed or dry granular
- ¼ cup lukewarm water
- 1 cup milk
- ¼ cup shortening
- ½ cup honey
- 1 teaspoon salt
- 2 eggs, beaten
- 1 cup currants or candied orange peel
- 1 teaspoon cinnamon
- ¼ teaspoon allspice
- 6 cups sifted enriched flour (about)

Soften yeast in lukewarm water. Scald milk. Add shortening, honey, and salt. Cool to lukewarm. Add flour to make a thick batter. Add yeast and eggs. Beat well. Add currants, spices and enough flour to make a soft dough. Turn out on lightly-floured board and knead until satiny. Place in greased bowl, cover and let rise until doubled in bulk. When light, shape into small buns and place on greased baking sheet or in pan. With knife or scissors, cut a small cross in the top of each bun. Let rise until doubled in bulk. Bake in moderate oven (375° F.) 20 to 25 minutes. While hot, ice with uncooked icing, following the cross cut in the buns. Yield: 3 dozen buns.

Holiday Bread

2½ cups sifted enriched flour
4 teaspoons baking powder
¼ cup sugar
1½ teaspoons salt
¼ cup chopped candied citron
¼ cup currants
2 tablespoons chopped candied lemon peel
2 tablespoons chopped candied cherries
½ cup chopped nuts
1 egg, beaten
½ cup honey
1 cup milk
¼ cup melted shortening

Sift together flour, baking powder, sugar, and salt. Add fruit and nuts. Combine egg, honey, milk and shortening. Add the egg mixture to the flour mixture, stirring only enough to moisten flour. Pour into greased loaf pan, 4½x8½-inches. Bake in moderate oven (375° F.) 1 hour to 1¼ hours. Yield: 1 1-pound loaf.

Honey Orange Rolls

2 packages yeast, compressed or dry granular
¼ cup lukewarm water
1 cup milk
¼ cup shortening
¼ cup sugar
¼ cup honey
1½ teaspoons salt
2 eggs, beaten
5 cups sifted enriched flour (about)

Filling:
¼ cup honey
2 tablespoons grated orange rind

Soften yeast in lukewarm water. Scald milk. Add shortening, sugar, honey, and salt. Cool to lukewarm. Add 2 cups flour, mixing well. Add softened yeast and eggs. Mix thoroughly. Add remaining flour to make a soft dough. Turn out on lightly-floured board and knead until smooth and satiny. Place in greased bowl, cover and let rise until doubled. Punch down. Let rest 10 minutes. Roll out into rectangular sheet ¼ inch thick and about 9 inches wide. Spread with honey. Sprinkle grated orange rind evenly over honey. Roll up jelly-roll fashion, sealing edges. Cut into 1-inch slices. Place slices cut side down into well-greased muffin pans. Cover and let rise until doubled. Bake in moderate oven (375° F.) 20 to 25 minutes. Yield: 3½ dozen rolls.

Date Nut Bread

1   cup boiling water
1   cup chopped dates
2   tablespoons shortening
¾   cup honey
1   egg
1½ cups enriched flour
¾   teaspoon salt
2   teaspoons baking powder
1   cup broken nut meats

Add boiling water to chopped dates and cook about two minutes stirring constantly. Cream shortening. Add honey gradually, beating well. Add egg and beat. Add date mixture. Add sifted dry ingredients and nuts. Mix well. Pour mixture into greased loaf pan 4½x8½ inches. Bake at 325° F. for 1 hour and 15 minutes, or until done. Yield: 1 loaf.

Sweet Biscuits

2   cups sifted flour
2   teaspoons baking powder
¾   teaspoon salt
4   tablespoons shortening
¾   cup milk
4   tablespoons butter
½   cup honey

Sift dry ingredients. Cut in shortening. Add milk gradually, stir to form soft dough. Place on lightly-floured board and knead for a few seconds. Roll ½ inch thick and cut with a floured biscuit cutter. Bake on ungreased baking sheet in hot oven (450° F.) about 15 minutes. When done, remove from oven, split biscuits in halves, spread lower half with butter and upper half with honey. Put together. Yield: 1 dozen biscuits.

Refrigerator Rolls

2   cakes yeast, compressed or dry granular
¼   cup lukewarm water
1   cup milk
½   cup honey
1   tablespoon salt
2   eggs
½   cup melted shortening
6   cups sifted enriched flour

Soften yeast in lukewarm water. Scald milk, add honey and salt. Add half the flour and beat well. Add softened yeast and beaten eggs. Mix well. Add shortening and remaining flour to make a soft dough. Knead until smooth. Place in greased bowl. Cover and place in refrigerator. When ready to bake, punch down dough and shape into rolls. Place rolls in greased pans. Cover and let rise until double in bulk. Bake in moderately-hot oven (425° F.) 15 to 20 minutes, or until done. Yield: 2½ dozen rolls.

Corn Sticks

2 ½ teaspoons baking powder
1 teaspoon salt
1 ¼ cups sifted flour
1 cup corn meal
2 eggs
1 ¼ cups milk
3 tablespoons honey
¼ cup melted shortening

Add baking powder and salt to sifted flour and sift again. Add corn meal and mix well. Combine well-beaten eggs, milk, honey and melted shortening. Add to dry ingredients; mix well. Bake in well-greased bread stick pans in hot oven (425° F.) 25 minutes, or until done. Yield: 3 dozen small corn sticks.

Honey Flake Gems

1 cup sifted flour
1 teaspoon salt
3 teaspoons baking powder
1 egg
¼ cup honey
½ cup milk
4 tablespoons melted fat
2 cups wheat flakes or corn flakes

Sift flour, salt, and baking powder together. Beat egg until light, add honey and milk, and stir into dry ingredients being careful not to overmix. Add slightly-cooled fat and stir just enough to mix ingredients. Carefully fold in cereal flakes. Fill greased muffin cups two-thirds full. Bake about 25 minutes in a moderate oven (350° F.). Yield: 10 medium-sized muffins or 12 small muffins.

Christmas Bread

1 package yeast, compressed or dry granular
¼ cup lukewarm water
½ cup honey
1 cup milk, scalded
4 cups sifted enriched flour
½ cup shortening, melted
2 eggs
2 teaspoons salt
1 cup raisins
½ cup cut citron
½ cup broken nut meats
½ cup cut candied cherries

Soften yeast in lukewarm water, add honey to milk. When lukewarm, add yeast and 2 cups flour. Mix well. Let stand in warm place until double in bulk. Add melted shortening, beaten eggs, and salt. Dredge cut fruit and nut meats in part of remaining flour. Add rest of flour and beat well. Place in greased bowl, cover and let stand until double in bulk. Remove from bowl and place on lightly-floured board. Punch down, cover with cloth and allow to stand for 10 minutes. Shape into ring in well-greased tube pan and let rise again until double in bulk. Bake in moderate oven (375° F.) about 30 to 35 minutes. Frost if desired.

Breads 61

Fruited Honey Wedding Cakes

TOAST TO THE BRIDE

May your happy honeymoon
Stay with you from June to June;
May you fly on fairy trips,
Honey ever on your lips;
May your larder always be
Stored with jars of pure honey
While your guests enjoy as treat,—
Nature's purest golden sweet.

H. M. G.

Wedding Reception

*Fruit Punch**
Assorted Canapés and Hors d'Oeuvres
*Ice Cream Molds   Fruited Honey Wedding Cake**
Fondant Patties   Salted Nuts

Fruited Honey Wedding Cake

Preparations. Have the shortening at room temperature. Grease and lightly flour 9-inch tube pan. Start oven for moderate heat (350° F.). Sift flour once before measuring.

Measurements

Measure into sifter:
- 3½ cups sifted cake flour
- 4 teaspoons double-acting baking powder
- 1½ teaspoons salt
- ½ cup sugar

Measure into bowl:
- 1 cup shortening

Mix in small bowl:
- 1 cup milk
- ⅔ cup honey
- 2 teaspoons almond extract

Have ready:
- 6 egg whites, beaten to meringue with ½ cup sugar*
- 1 cup finely-chopped candied cherries
- ½ cup finely-chopped citron
- 1½ cups chopped nut meats.

* Make meringue by beating 6 egg whites with rotary egg beater (or at high speed of electric mixer) until foamy. Add ½ cup sugar gradually, beating only until meringue holds up in soft peaks.

Now the Mix-Easy Part

(Mix by hand or at a low speed of electric mixer.) Stir shortening just to soften. Sift in dry ingredients. Add liquid and mix until all flour is dampened. Then *beat 2 minutes*. Add meringue mixture and *beat 1 minute* longer. Fold in fruits and nuts. (Count only actual beating time or count beating strokes. Allow about 150 full strokes per minute. Scrape bowl and spoon often.)

Baking. Turn batter into pan. Bake in moderate oven (350° F.) 75 minutes, or until done. Cool ½ hour. Remove from pan and spread Honeymoon Frosting on top and sides of cake.

Honeymoon Frosting

Beat 1 egg white with dash of salt until stiff enough to hold up in peaks, but not dry. Pour ½ cup honey in fine stream over egg white, beating constantly about 4 minutes, or until frosting holds its shape. (This is a delicate frosting and does not store well overnight. Cake should be frosted the day it is served.)

Cakes

Brownstone Front Cake

Preparations. Have the shortening at room temperature. Line bottom of 10x10x2-inch pan with paper, then grease. Start oven for moderate heat (350° F.). Sift flour once before measuring.

Measurements

Measure into sifter:	*Measure into mixing bowl:*
2½ cups sifted cake flour	¼ cup shortening
1 teaspoon soda	*Mix in small bowl:*
1 teaspoon salt	¼ cup sour milk or buttermilk
1 teaspoon cinnamon	¼ cup honey
½ teaspoon nutmeg	
½ teaspoon allspice	

Have ready:
 ¾ cup brown sugar, firmly packed
 3 eggs, unbeaten
 1 cup finely-chopped nut meats
 1 cup raisins, cooked, drained, and finely chopped

Now the Mix-Easy Part

(Mix by hand or at a low speed of electric mixer.) Stir shortening just to soften. Sift in dry ingredients. Add brown sugar. (Force through sieve to remove lumps, if necessary.) Add ½ cup of the liquid and eggs. Mix until all flour is dampened. Then *beat 1 minute.* Add remaining liquid, nuts, and raisins, blend, and *beat 2 minutes* longer.

Baking. Turn batter into pan and bake in a moderate oven (350° F.) 55 minutes, or until done.

Honey Nut Cake

2 cups sifted cake flour
2 teaspoons baking powder
½ teaspoon salt
⅔ cup butter or other shortening
½ cup sugar
½ cup honey
3 eggs
1 cup finely-cut nut meats
¼ cup milk
1 teaspoon vanilla

Sift flour once, measure, add baking powder and salt, and sift together three times. Cream shortening, add sugar gradually, and cream thoroughly; then add honey in thirds, beating well after each addition. Add ¼ of flour and beat until smooth and well blended. Beat eggs until thick enough to pile up in bowl; add to cake mixture and beat well. Add nuts. Add remaining flour in thirds, alternately with milk in halves, beating very well after each addition. Add vanilla. Bake in greased 9x5x3-inch loaf pan in slow oven (325° F.) 1 hour and 25 minutes, or until done. Frost if desired.

Honey Spice Cake

2	cups sifted cake flour
2	teaspoons baking powder
¾	teaspoon salt
1½	teaspoons allspice
½	cup shortening
1	teaspoon grated lemon rind
¾	cup honey
2	egg yolks, unbeaten
½	cup milk
⅔	cup chopped raisins
1	teaspoon vanilla
2	egg whites
⅓	cup chopped walnut meats

Sift flour once, measure, add baking powder, salt, and allspice, and sift together three times. Cream shortening with lemon rind; add honey gradually, beating well after each addition. Add ¼ of flour and beat until smooth and well blended. Add yolks, one at a time, beating well after each. Add remaining flour in thirds, alternately with milk in halves, beating very well after each addition. Add raisins with last addition of flour. Add vanilla. Beat egg whites until they will hold up in moist peaks. Stir quickly but thoroughly into batter. Turn into greased 8x8x2-inch pan and sprinkle with nut meats. Bake in moderate oven (350° F.) 55 minutes, or until done or in two greased 8-inch layer pans in moderate oven (375° F.) 25 minutes, or until done.

Honey Ginger Cake

2½	cups sifted cake flour
2	teaspoons soda
1	teaspoon salt
1	teaspoon ground ginger
1	teaspoon ground cinnamon
½	cup shortening
½	cup brown sugar, firmly packed
1	egg, unbeaten
1	cup honey
1	cup sour milk or buttermilk

Sift flour once, measure, add soda, salt, and spices, and sift together three times. Cream shortening thoroughly, add sugar gradually, and cream together until light and fluffy. Add egg and beat very thoroughly. Add honey and blend. Add flour, alternately with sour milk, a small amount at a time, beating after each addition until smooth. Bake in two well-greased 9-inch layer pans in moderate oven (350° F.) 45 minutes, or until done.

Remarks: Honey Ginger Cake may be baked in paper-lined cupcake pans in moderate oven (350° F.) 35 minutes, or until done. Delicious served plain, or topped with whipped cream and chopped black walnuts.

Quick Frosting for Cake

1	cup chocolate, broken or cut in pieces
¾	cup peanut butter
¼	cup honey
2	tablespoons water

Melt chocolate. Combine peanut butter, honey and water. Add chocolate. Stir until smooth.

Honey Orange Cake

½ cup shortening
½ cup sugar
½ cup honey
1 egg
2 cups all-purpose enriched flour
2 teaspoons baking powder
¼ teaspoon soda
¼ teaspoon salt
½ cup finely-shredded orange peel
¼ cup orange juice
1 teaspoon grated lemon rind or lemon flavoring

Cream shortening. Add sugar gradually, add honey, creaming constantly. Beat in egg. Sift dry ingredients thoroughly (flour, baking powder, soda, salt); add orange peel. Combine orange juice and flavoring. Add dry ingredients and orange juice alternately to creamed mixture beginning and ending with flour mixture. Spread in well-greased cake pan, 8x8x2-inches. (Mixture is quite thick.) Bake in moderate oven (350° F.) about 45 to 60 minutes. Let stand 7 or 8 minutes before removing cake from pan. Serve plain, iced, or with hot fruit sauce, warm or cold. Yield: 16 two-inch squares.
Honey Orange Sauce: Blend ½ cup orange juice with ⅓ cup honey. Pass sauce or pour over the warm or cold cake.

Honey Devil's Food Cake (Red)

1½ cups sifted cake flour
1 teaspoon soda
¼ teaspoon salt
4 tablespoons butter or other shortening
½ cup sugar
½ cup honey
1 egg, unbeaten
2 squares unsweetened chocolate, melted
¾ cup sour milk or buttermilk
1 teaspoon vanilla

Sift flour once, measure, add soda and salt, and sift together three times. Cream shortening, add sugar gradually, and cream together well. Add honey gradually and beat thoroughly. Add ¼ of the flour and beat well. Add egg and beat very thoroughly; then add chocolate and blend. Add remainder of flour, alternately with milk, a small amount at a time, beating after each addition until smooth. Add vanilla. Bake in two greased 8-inch layer pans in moderate oven (350° F.) 25 minutes, or until done. Spread Easy Fluffy Honey Frosting on tops and sides of cake. This cake may be baked in greased cupcake pans in moderate oven (350° F.) 20 minutes, or until done. Yield: 2½ dozen medium cupcakes.

Honey Fudge Cake

Preparations. Have shortening at room temperature. Grease two 9-inch layer pans or 10x10x2-inch pan, cover bottoms with waxed paper, and grease again. Start oven for moderate heat (350° F.). Sift flour once before measuring.

Measurements

Measure into sifter:
    2 cups sifted cake flour
    1½ teaspoons soda
    1 teaspoon salt
Measure into bowl:
    ½ cup shortening

Mix in small bowl:
    1¼ cups honey
    ⅔ cup water
    1 teaspoon vanilla
Have ready:
    2 eggs, unbeaten
    2½ squares unsweetened chocolate, melted

Now the Mix-Easy Part

Mix shortening just to soften. Sift in dry ingredients. Add ½ cup of the liquid and the eggs. Mix until all flour is dampened; then *beat 1 minute.* Add remaining liquid and melted chocolate, blend, and *beat 2 minutes* longer. Batter will be thin. (Count only actual beating time or count beating strokes. Allow about 150 full strokes per minute. Scrape bowl and spoon or beater often.)

Baking. Turn batter into pans. Bake in moderate oven (350° F.) about 30 minutes for layers or about 40 minutes for square cake. Frost with Easy Fluffy Honey Frosting.

If desired, a square cake may be sprinkled with ½ cup coarsely-chopped nut meats before baking. Omit frosting.

Note: Mix cake by hand or at low speed of electric mixer.

Every Day Honey Cake

2 cups sifted cake flour
2 teaspoons baking powder
¼ teaspoon salt
⅓ cup shortening
½ cup sugar
½ cup honey
1 egg, unbeaten
½ cup milk
1 teaspoon vanilla extract

Sift dry ingredients together three times. Cream shortening, add sugar gradually and cream until light and fluffy. Add honey gradually, beating after each addition. Add ½ cup of sifted dry ingredients. Beat well. Add egg and beat thoroughly. Add remainder of dry ingredients alternately with milk, beating after each addition. Add vanilla extract. Bake in two layers in greased pans in moderate oven (375° F.) 20 to 25 minutes. Spread jelly between layers. Cover top of cake with honey-sweetened whipped cream.

Cakes

Fudge Nut Cake

Preparations. Have shortening at room temperature. Grease 13x9x2-inch pan, line bottom with waxed paper, and grease again. Start oven for moderate heat (375° F.). Sift flour once before measuring.

Measurements

Measure into sifter:
  2   cups sifted cake flour
  1   teaspoon soda
  ¾ teaspoon salt

Have ready:
  ¾ cup brown sugar, firmly packed
  2   eggs, unbeaten
  3   squares unsweetened chocolate, melted
  1   cup coarsely-chopped nut meats

Measure into bowl:
  ½ cup vegetable shortening
Mix in small bowl:
  ¼ cup honey
  1   cup milk
  1   teaspoon vanilla

Now the Mix-Easy Part

(Mix cake by hand or at low speed of electric mixer.) Mix shortening just to soften. Sift in dry ingredients. Add brown sugar (force through sieve to remove lumps, if necessary). Add ½ of the liquid and the eggs. Mix until all flour is dampened; then *beat 1 minute.* Add remaining liquid; blend. Then add chocolate and *beat 2 minutes* longer. Add nuts. (Count only actual beating time or count beating strokes. Allow about 150 full strokes per minute. Scrape bowl and spoon or beater often.)
Baking. Turn batter into pan. Bake in moderate oven (375° F.) 35 minutes, or until done.
This cake may be baked in greased and floured 9-inch tube pan in moderate oven (350° F.) 1 hour and 10 minutes, or until done.

Special Chocolate Frosting

½ cup sugar
¼ cup butter
¼ cup light cream
¼ cup honey
¼ teaspoon salt
3 squares unsweetened chocolate, cut into small pieces
2 egg yolks, well beaten

Combine sugar, butter, cream, honey, salt, and chocolate in top of double boiler. Place over boiling water. When chocolate is melted, beat with rotary beater until blended. Pour small amount of mixture over egg yolks, stirring vigorously. Return to double boiler and cook 2 minutes longer, or until mixture thickens slightly, stirring constantly. Remove from hot water, place in pan of ice water or cracked ice, and beat until of right consistency to spread. Yield: Frosting to cover tops and sides of 2 8-inch layers.

All Honey Chocolate Cake

2 cups sifted cake flour
1½ teaspoons soda
½ teaspoon salt
½ cup shortening
1¼ cups honey
2 eggs, unbeaten
3 squares unsweetened chocolate, melted
⅔ cup water
1 teaspoon vanilla

Sift flour once, measure, add soda and salt, and sift together three times. Cream butter, add honey very gradually, by tablespoons at first, beating very hard after each addition to keep mixture thick. Add ¼ of flour and beat until smooth and well blended. Add eggs, one at a time, beating well after each. Add chocolate and blend. Add remaining flour in thirds, alternately with water in halves, beating very well after each addition. Add vanilla. Bake in two greased 9-inch layer pans in moderate oven (350° F.) 30 minutes, or until done. Spread Easy Fluffy Honey Frosting between layers and on top of cake.

Note: For best results, beat *very* well at each stage of mixing.

Easy Fluffy Honey Frosting

1 egg white
Dash of salt
½ cup honey

Beat egg white with salt until stiff enough to hold up in peaks, but not dry. Pour honey in fine stream over egg white, beating constantly until frosting holds its shape. (Beat about 2½ minutes with electric mixer, or about 4 minutes by hand.) Yield: About 2¼ cups frosting, or enough to cover tops of two 8-inch layers or top and sides of 8x8x2-inch cake. If desired, decorate frosting with Bittersweet Coating dribbled from teaspoon.

Honey Orange Icing (Uncooked)

1 egg white
⅛ teaspoon salt
½ cup honey
½ teaspoon grated orange rind

Add salt to egg white. Warm honey over hot water. Pour in a thin stream over egg white while beating vigorously. Add orange rind and continue to beat until thick and fluffy. Spread on cake. Sprinkle with extra grated orange rind. Yield: About 2 cups frosting.

Honey Fudge Cupcakes

2 cups sifted cake flour
1½ teaspoons soda
1 teaspoon salt
1¼ cups honey
⅔ cup water
1 teaspoon vanilla
½ cup shortening
2 eggs, unbeaten
2½ squares unsweetened chocolate, melted
½ cup chopped nut meats

Sift flour once; measure into sifter with soda and salt. Combine honey, water, and vanilla. Have shortening at room temperature; mix just to soften. Sift in dry ingredients. Add ½ cup of the liquid and the eggs. Mix until all flour is dampened; then *beat 1 minute.* Add remaining liquid and melted chocolate, blend, and *beat 2 minutes* longer. (Batter will be thin.) Turn into well-greased cupcake pans, filling pans only ½ full. Sprinkle nuts over batter. Bake in moderate oven (350° F.) 25 minutes, or until done. Let cool about 10 minutes before removing from pan. Yield: 2 dozen large or 2½ dozen medium cupcakes.
Note: Mix by hand or at low speed of electric mixer. Count only actual beating time or count beating strokes. Allow about 150 full strokes per minute. Scrape bowl and spoon or beater often.

Honey Angel Food

1 teaspoon cream of tartar
½ teaspoon salt
1 cup egg whites (8 to 10 whites)
¾ cup sugar
1 cup cake flour
½ cup honey
½ teaspoon grated lemon rind

Add the cream of tartar and salt to the egg whites in a bowl. Beat the whites with a wire whip until they are stiff. They should move only slightly when the bowl is tipped. Fold one-half the sugar slowly into the egg whites 2 tablespoons at a time. Sift the remaining sugar with the flour and add later. The ½ cup honey must be warmed so that it will be thin and will pour in a fine stream over the egg whites as the egg whites are folded in. After the honey is added, fold in the flour and sugar mixture, sifting ¼ cup over the whites at a time. Add grated lemon rind. Pour the mixture into an angel food pan and bake at a temperature of 300° F. for 50 minutes. Invert the pan, cool and remove to a cake rack.

Honey Fruit Cake

1 pound seeded raisins
½ pound cooked prunes (cut in small pieces)
½ pound candied citron
¼ pound candied orange peel
¼ pound candied lemon peel
¼ pound candied cherries
½ pound almonds
½ cup orange juice
1 cup prune juice
1 cup honey
1 cup shortening
1½ cups brown sugar
4 eggs
4 cups sifted flour
1 teaspoon baking powder
1 teaspoon salt
¼ teaspoon baking soda
1 teaspoon mace
2 teaspoons cinnamon
½ teaspoon cloves
½ teaspoon nutmeg
½ teaspoon allspice

Prepare the fruit the day before baking the cake. Place fruit in large bowl, cover with fruit juices and honey and allow to stand overnight. Cream shortening well. Add brown sugar and cream until light. Add well-beaten eggs and mix well. Add part of the sifted dry ingredients, fruit, and almonds (blanched and cut). Mix well. Add remainder of sifted dry ingredients. Mix well. Line pans with brown paper. Grease paper. Put cake mixture in pan and bake in a slow oven (275° F.) for about 3 hours. Yield: 2 three-pound cakes.

Duchess Cake

¼ cup fat
½ cup sugar
1 egg
½ cup honey
½ cup milk
2 tablespoons orange juice
1 teaspoon grated orange rind
1½ cups sifted flour
¼ teaspoon soda
1 teaspoon baking powder
¼ teaspoon salt
¼ teaspoon cinnamon
⅛ teaspoon ginger
½ cup wheat and barley kernels

Cream fat and sugar together; add egg and beat until light and fluffy. Add honey, milk, orange juice, and rind. Sift flour with soda, baking powder, salt and spices, mix in cereal and add to first mixture. Combine well, but do not overbeat. Pour into a pan with the bottom lined with waxed paper. Bake in a moderate oven (350° F.) for 35 minutes, or until done. Yield: 1 cake (8x8x2-inch).

Chocolate Honey Angel Food Cake

¾ cup sifted cake flour
¼ cup cocoa
1 cup sifted granulated sugar
1 cup egg whites (8 to 10 whites)
¼ teaspoon salt
¾ teaspoon cream of tartar
1 teaspoon vanilla extract
⅓ cup honey

Sift flour once, measure, add cocoa and ¼ cup of the sugar, and sift together 4 times. Beat egg whites and salt with rotary beater or flat wire whisk. When foamy, add cream of tartar and vanilla. Continue beating until eggs are stiff enough to hold up in peaks, but not dry. Add remaining ¾ cup of sugar, 2 tablespoons at a time, beating after each addition until sugar is just blended. Add honey, 2 tablespoons at a time, beating after each addition until honey is just blended. Sift about ¼ cup flour-sugar mixture over egg whites and fold in lightly; repeat until all flour is used. Turn into ungreased angel food pan. Cut gently through batter with knife to remove air bubbles. Bake in slow oven (325° F.) 1 hour. Remove from oven and invert pan 1 hour, or until cold.

Cherry Nut Loaf Cake

1¾ cups sifted cake flour
2 teaspoons baking powder
¾ teaspoon salt
¼ cup sugar
3 egg whites
¼ cup sugar
½ cup shortening
½ cup milk
⅓ cup honey
1 teaspoon almond extract
½ cup finely-chopped candied cherries
¼ cup finely-chopped citron
1 cup chopped nut meats

Sift flour once, measure into sifter with baking powder, salt and ¼ cup sugar. Beat egg whites until foamy. Add ¼ cup sugar gradually, beating only until mixture will stand in soft peaks; set aside. Have shortening at room temperature; mix or stir just to soften. Sift in dry ingredients. Add milk, honey, and almond extract and mix until all flour is dampened. Then *beat 2 minutes*. Add egg white mixture and *beat 1 minute* longer. Fold in fruit and nuts. (Mix cake by hand or at a low speed of electric mixer. Count only actual beating time or count beating strokes. Allow about 150 full strokes per minute. Scrape bowl and spoon often while mixing.) Turn into 9x5x3-inch loaf pan which has been lined on bottom with paper, then greased. Bake in moderate oven (350° F.) 65 minutes, or until done. Let stand overnight before slicing.

Fruit Cake

1 cup shortening
½ cup sugar
½ cup honey
5 eggs
1½ cups flour
1 teaspoon salt
1 teaspoon baking powder
1 teaspoon cinnamon
½ teaspoon nutmeg
½ teaspoon cloves
½ teaspoon mace
¼ cup orange juice
½ pound seeded raisins
¼ pound cut citron
¼ pound cut, candied pineapple
½ pound cut, candied cherries
¼ pound cut, candied orange peel
¼ pound cut, candied lemon peel
½ pound halved, blanched almond nut meats
½ pound cut, pitted dates
¼ cup flour (to dredge fruits)

Cream shortening and sugar, add honey and beat well. Add well-beaten eggs, beat thoroughly. Add sifted dry ingredients alternately with orange juice. Beat well. Dredge fruits and nuts with ¼ cup flour. Add to batter. Mix well. Line pans with greased brown paper. Pour batter into pans. Cover cakes with greased brown paper. Bake in slow oven (250° F.) about 3½ hours. Cool 5 minutes. Remove cakes to cooling rack. When thoroughly cool, store in covered container in cool place. Yield: About 5 pounds.

Honey Almond Frosting

2 egg whites, unbeaten
¾ cup honey
1 cup chopped almonds, toasted

Place egg whites and honey in top of double boiler, beating with rotary egg beater until thoroughly mixed. Place over rapidly boiling water, beat constantly with rotary egg beater, and cook 7 minutes, or until frosting will stand in peaks. Remove from boiling water; add ½ of nuts. Spread on cake, sprinkling remaining nuts over top of cake while frosting is still soft. Yield: Enough frosting to cover tops and sides of two 8-inch layers (generously) or tops and sides of two 9-inch layers.

Candies

Children's Party
Individual Casseroles
(Chicken, Peas, and Noodles)
Butterfly Salad*   *Honey-Lemon Dressing**
Circus Sandwiches*
Pink Ice Cream   *Angel Food Cake**
Milk

Caramel Apples

6 medium apples
1 cup sugar
¾ cup honey
1 cup light cream
2 tablespoons butter
1 teaspoon vanilla

Stick wooden skewers in stem end of apples. Combine sugar, honey, cream and butter. Cook over low heat until sugar dissolves. Cook to very hard stage (256° to 260° F.) without stirring. Remove from heat. Add vanilla. Dip apples in sirup, working fast. Roll in coarsely-chopped nut meats. Place on well-greased cooky sheet to cool.

Honey Nougat

1 cup sugar
½ cup honey
½ cup water
2 egg whites
¼ teaspoon salt
¾ cup chopped almonds
½ cup Pistachio nuts
¼ cup candied cherries
1 teaspoon vanilla extract

Mix sugar, honey and water in top of double boiler. Cook slowly stirring only until sugar is dissolved. Then cook until brittle in cold water (300° F.). Pour sirup over the stiffly-beaten egg whites beating constantly. Fold in salt, nuts, cherries and vanilla. Return mixture to double boiler and cook, stirring constantly until it will hold its shape when dropped from a spoon. It should not be sticky to touch. Pour into a greased pan. Let stand a day before cutting. Cut and wrap in waxed paper.

Honey-Glazed Pecans

½ cup honey
24 pecan halves

Boil honey to firm ball stage (250° F.). Cool. Dip pecan halves into mixture. Place on waxed paper to set.

Stuffed Dates

Slit dates on one side with sharp knife. Remove pit. Fill with one of the following fillings:

Dried Apricots and Honey:
Put ½ cup dried apricots and ½ cup walnuts through fine knife of food chopper. Add ¼ cup honey and blend well.

Peanut Butter and Honey:
Combine ¼ cup peanut butter and 2 tablespoons honey. Blend well.

Nut-Raisin-Honey:
Put ½ cup seeded raisins, ½ cup Brazil nuts through food chopper, using fine knife. Add honey to moisten. Blend well.

Honey Scotch

½ cup water
2 cups sugar
½ cup honey

Heat water and sugar stirring until sugar is dissolved. Add honey and cook, stirring gently just enough to prevent scorching. Cook to the hard crack stage or 300° F. Remove cooking utensil from heat and pour candy into a buttered pan. When candy begins to set, cut into strips 1-inch wide. Roll into cylinders. Cut with a scissors into pieces 1-inch long. Yield: 1 pound.

Popcorn Balls

1 cup honey
1 cup sugar
½ cup water
1 teaspoon salt
1 teaspoon vanilla extract

Combine honey, sugar, water and salt in sauce pan. Place over low heat stirring until mixture begins to boil. Cook to firm ball stage (248° F.). Remove from heat. Add vanilla and stir only to blend well. Pour slowly over 3 quarts popped corn in large bowl. Rinse hands in cold water or lightly grease hands and press popped corn into balls. Wrap in waxed paper. To make pink popcorn balls, use pink coloring according to directions on package. Omit vanilla extract. Yield: 8 medium popcorn balls.

Chocolate-Topped Toffee

⅓ cup melted butter or margarine
2 cups rolled oats (quick or regular)
½ cup brown sugar
¼ cup honey
½ teaspoon salt
1½ teaspoons vanilla
1 cup (4-ounces) semi-sweet chocolate (chips or pieces)
¼ cup finely-chopped nuts

Pour melted shortening over rolled oats, mixing thoroughly. Add brown sugar, honey, salt, and vanilla; mix until combined. Pack firmly into well-greased 8-inch square pan. Bake in hot oven (450° F.) for about 12 minutes, or until a rich brown color. (Mixture will be bubbling.) Place on wire rack and let stand until completely cold. Loosen the edges, turn pan over and strike firmly against table top until candy is loosened. Melt chocolate over hot water and spread on top of candy. Sprinkle with finely-chopped nuts. Chill in refrigerator until chocolate hardens. Cut in small squares or bars. Yield: 64 candies, 1-inch square.

Note: ½ square bitter chocolate may be added with semi-sweet chocolate.

Honey Fudge

2 cups sugar
1 square unsweetened chocolate
¼ teaspoon salt
1 cup evaporated milk
¼ cup honey
2 tablespoons butter
1 cup nuts

Boil sugar, chocolate, salt, and milk for five minutes. Add honey and cook to soft-ball stage (240° F.). Add butter; let stand until lukewarm; beat until creamy, add nuts, and pour into buttered pan. Cut when firm.

Confitures

Buffet Luncheon

Baked Crab Meat and Shrimp
Assorted Relishes
Honey Tea Biscuits*
Ice Cream*
Coffee
Nuts   Candies

Plum Butter

5 pounds plums
Water
Honey

Pick over and wash plums. Remove blemishes. Put in kettle and cover with water. Cook until tender. Put through colander to remove skins and pits. Measure plum pulp and add ½ cup honey for each cup of pulp. Mix well. Cook until thick. Seal in hot, sterilized jars.

Rhubarb Jelly

2 cups rhubarb juice
½ cup water
4 tablespoons granulated pectin
2 cups honey

Wash rhubarb and cut into 1-inch lengths, retain skin. Place in preserving kettle. Add ½ cup water to prevent rhubarb from sticking to kettle. Cover and cook over low heat until soft. Drain through jelly bag. Measure juice. Place juice in kettle. Add pectin and stir vigorously. Bring to boil. Add honey and continue to boil until jelly test is reached, about 224° F. Pour into sterilized jelly glasses. Cover with paraffin.

Beet Pickles

1 cup cider vinegar
1 cup water
1 cup honey
2 teaspoons mustard seed
1 teaspoon whole allspice
1 teaspoon whole cloves
1 stick cinnamon
1 teaspoon salt

Place vinegar and water in preserving kettle. Heat to boiling point. Add honey and salt. Stir well. Add spices which have been tied in a small piece of muslin. Cook 5 minutes. Add small beets that have been cooked and skinned. Allow to simmer 20 minutes. Seal in sterilized jars.

Fig Preserves

2 quarts figs
2 cups honey
2 cups sugar
3 cups water
Several slices of lemon rind cooked in ½ cup water, if desired.

Select the best figs, thoroughly ripe, but not soft. Leave about ½ inch stem on figs. Sprinkle figs with ⅓ cup soda and 5 cups boiling water. Let stand for 5 minutes to remove fuzzy outer layer of skin. Rinse thoroughly and drain well, or dry. Boil sugar, honey, and water together for 10 minutes before adding figs. Add figs slowly in order to keep sirup boiling gently. When all figs have been added, boil in covered kettle until figs are clear. Skim and let stand overnight. Drain off sirup and boil until thick. Pack figs into sterilized containers and fill with boiling sirup. Seal at once and store in cool place. Yield: About 2½ pints.

Use a large kettle when making jelly or jam in which part or all honey is used.

Since honey contains some moisture, it is necessary to cook the mixture somewhat longer in order to obtain the desired consistency.

Cookies

Sunday Brunch
All Year Fresh Fruit Cup*
Cheese Baked Eggs on Toast Rounds
Broiled Sausages
Honey Kuchen*
Coffee

Lemon Honey Drop Cookies

1½ cups sifted flour
1½ teaspoons baking powder
½ cup shortening
¼ cup honey
1 tablespoon lemon juice
1 egg

Sift flour and baking powder. Cream shortening and honey thoroughly. Add lemon juice. Add egg yolk. Beat well. Add dry ingredients. Fold in stiffly-beaten egg white. Drop by teaspoon on greased cooky sheet. Bake in hot oven (425° F.) about 12 minutes. Yield: About 2½ dozen cookies.

Fruit-Filled Cookies

1 cup shortening
1 cup brown sugar
1 cup honey
3 eggs
4 cups sifted flour
1 teaspoon cinnamon
1 teaspoon soda
½ teaspoon salt

Cream shortening. Add sugar and cream well. Add honey gradually and continue creaming. Add eggs, one at a time, beating well after each. Add sifted dry ingredients. Divide dough into two parts. Roll each about ¼ inch thick. Cover dough with the following filling. Roll like jelly roll. Wrap each roll in waxed paper. Place in refrigerator overnight. Slice thin. Bake in moderate oven (375° F.) about 12 minutes. Yield: About 50 cookies.

Filling

1 cup dates, pitted and cut
½ cup honey
¼ cup water
1 teaspoon lemon juice
½ cup nuts, chopped

Cook dates, honey and water until dates are soft. Remove from heat. Add lemon juice and nuts. Cool.

Honey Drops

¼ cup shortening
½ cup honey
1 egg
1 cup rolled oats
1 tablespoon milk
1 cup sifted flour
3 teaspoons baking powder
¼ teaspoon salt
½ teaspoon cinnamon
½ cup raisins

Cream shortening and honey together thoroughly. Add egg and beat until blended. Stir in rolled oats and milk. Sift dry ingredients, add with raisins and mix well. Drop by teaspoon on greased baking sheet. Bake in moderately hot oven (375° F.) 20 to 25 minutes. Yield: 2½ dozen cookies.

Honey Raisin Bars

1⅓ cups sifted flour
½ teaspoon salt
1 teaspoon baking powder
3 eggs
1 cup honey
1 cup broken nut meats
1 cup raisins, chopped

Mix and sift dry ingredients. Beat eggs well. Add honey and mix thoroughly. Add nut meats and raisins. Add sifted dry ingredients gradually. Mix lightly, just to combine ingredients. Spread mixture in well-greased pan. Bake in moderate oven (350° F.) 35 to 40 minutes. When slightly cool cut into bars. Yield: 4 dozen bars.

Lebkuchen

4 cups sifted cake flour
¼ teaspoon soda
¾ teaspoon cinnamon
⅛ teaspoon cloves
⅛ teaspoon nutmeg
⅔ cup honey (½ pound)
½ cup brown sugar, firmly packed
2 tablespoons water
1 egg, slightly beaten
¾ cup (3 ounces) shredded candied orange peel
¾ cup (3 ounces) shredded candied citron
1 cup almonds, blanched and shredded

Sift flour once, measure, add soda and spices, and sift together three times. Combine honey, sugar, and water and boil 5 minutes. Cool. Add flour, egg, fruits, and nuts. Press dough into a cake, wrap in waxed paper, and store in refrigerator 2 or 3 days to ripen. Roll ¼ inch thick on lightly-floured board. Cut in 1x3-inch strips. Bake on greased baking sheet in moderate oven (350° F.) 15 minutes. When cool, spread with Transparent Glaze. Store at least one day before serving. Yield: About 5 dozen cookies.

To make Transparent Glaze, see page 37.

Note: These cookies are characteristically hard and chewy. They develop a better flavor upon storage. Store two weeks or longer.

Honey Chocolate Chip Squares

½ cup sifted flour
¼ teaspoon soda
¼ teaspoon salt
⅓ cup honey
1 egg, well beaten
1 tablespoon melted shortening
1 package semi-sweet chocolate chips
⅔ cup chopped walnut meats
1 teaspoon vanilla

Sift flour once, measure, add soda and salt, and sift again. Add honey gradually to egg, beating thoroughly. Add shortening, chocolate chips, nuts, and vanilla, mixing thoroughly. Then add flour and mix well. Turn mixture into 8x8x2-inch pan which has been greased, lined with waxed paper, and again greased. Bake in slow oven (325° F.) 35 minutes, or until done. Cut in squares, remove from pan, and cool on cake rack. Yield: 20 squares.

Honey Fruit Cookies

8 cups sifted cake flour
½ teaspoon soda
1½ teaspoons cinnamon
¼ teaspoon cloves
¼ teaspoon nutmeg
1⅓ cups honey
1 cup brown sugar, firmly packed
¼ cup water
2 eggs, slightly beaten
1½ cups (6 ounces) candied orange peel, shredded
1½ cups (6 ounces) candied citron, shredded
2 cups (¾ pound) almonds, blanched and shredded

Sift flour once, measure, add soda and spices, and sift together three times. Boil honey, sugar, and water 5 minutes. Cool. Add flour, eggs, fruits, and nuts. Work into loaf and place in refrigerator. Let ripen 2 or 3 days. Roll ¼ inch thick on lightly-floured board. Cut in strips 1x3-inches. Bake on greased baking sheet in moderate oven (350° F.) 15 minutes. When cool, cover with Glaze. Yield: 10 dozen cookies.

To make Transparent Glaze, combine 2 cups sifted confectioners' sugar and 3 tablespoons boiling water. Add 1 teaspoon vanilla. Beat thoroughly. Spread on cookies while Glaze is still warm.

Honey Oatmeal Cookies

½ cup shortening
1 cup honey
1 egg, unbeaten
1½ cups sifted flour
½ teaspoon soda
½ teaspoon salt
1⅔ cups oatmeal
4 tablespoons sour milk
1 cup raisins
½ cup chopped peanuts

Cream shortening. Add the honey and blend. Stir in the egg. Sift together dry ingredients and add the oatmeal to this. Add dry ingredients alternately with milk to the shortening and honey mixture. Stir in nuts and raisins. Drop by spoonfuls on a greased pan or baking sheet. Bake in a moderate oven (350° F.) for 15 minutes. Yield: 3 dozen cookies.

Honey Icebox Cookies

2½ cups sifted flour
2 teaspoons baking powder
½ teaspoon salt
½ teaspoon cinnamon
½ cup chopped walnut meats
1 egg, well beaten
½ cup sugar
¼ teaspoon almond extract
½ cup honey
¾ cup melted shortening

Sift flour once, measure, add baking powder, salt, and cinnamon, and sift again. Add nuts. Combine egg, sugar, flavoring, honey and shortening; add to flour-nut mixture, mixing well. Shape in rolls, 1½ inches in diameter, and roll each in waxed paper. Chill overnight, or until firm enough to slice. Cut in ⅛-inch slices; bake on ungreased baking sheet in hot oven (400° F.) for 10 minutes. Yield: About 4 dozen cookies.

Brownies

⅔ cup sifted flour
½ teaspoon baking powder
¼ teaspoon salt
⅓ cup butter or other shortening
2 squares unsweetened chocolate
½ cup sugar
½ cup honey
2 eggs, well beaten
½ cup broken walnut meats
1 teaspoon vanilla

Sift flour once, measure, add baking powder and salt, and sift again. Melt shortening and chocolate over boiling water. Add sugar gradually to eggs, beating thoroughly. Add honey and chocolate mixture to egg mixture and blend. Add flour and mix well; then add nuts and vanilla. Bake in greased pan, 8x8x2-inches, in moderate oven (350° F.) 40 minutes. Cut in squares. Remove from pan and cool on cake rack. Yield: 2 dozen brownies.

Honey Chocolate Chip Cookies

⅓ cup shortening
½ cup honey
1 egg, well beaten
1¼ cups sifted flour
½ teaspoon salt
½ teaspoon soda
1 package semi-sweet chocolate chips
½ cup chopped nut meats
1 teaspoon vanilla

Cream shortening, add honey gradually, and cream together until light and fluffy. Add egg and mix thoroughly. Sift flour once, measure, add salt and soda, and sift again. Add flour in two parts and mix well. Add chocolate chips, nuts, and vanilla, and mix thoroughly. Drop from teaspoon on greased baking sheet 2 inches apart. Bake in moderate oven (375° F.) 10 to 12 minutes. Yield: About 4 dozen cookies.

Honey Chocolate Cookies

1 cup shortening
1¼ cups honey
2 eggs
2 squares chocolate, melted
2½ cups sifted flour
1 teaspoon baking powder
½ teaspoon salt
1 teaspoon cinnamon
¼ teaspoon cloves
1½ cups rolled oats
1 cup broken nut meats

Cream shortening, add honey gradually; beat well. Add well-beaten eggs, melted chocolate. Add sifted dry ingredients, rolled oats and nut meats. Mix well. Drop from teaspoon, 2 inches apart, on greased cooky sheets. Bake in moderate oven (325° F.) 15 minutes. Yield: 4 dozen cookies.

Honey Drop Cookies

⅔ cup shortening
1¼ cups honey
1 egg
1 teaspoon vanilla extract
2½ cups flour
3 teaspoons baking powder
¼ teaspoon salt
½ cup chopped walnut meats

Cream shortening, add honey gradually, beat well. Add well-beaten egg and vanilla. Add sifted dry ingredients and nut meats. Mix well. Drop from teaspoon, 2 inches apart, on greased cooky sheet. Bake in moderate oven (350° F.) 15 minutes. Yield: 4 dozen cookies.

Honey Peanut Butter Cookies

¼ cup shortening
½ cup peanut butter
½ cup sugar
½ cup honey
1 egg
2 cups sifted flour
1 teaspoon baking powder
¼ teaspoon soda
½ teaspoon salt
¾ cup chopped nut meats

Cream shortening and peanut butter together. Add sugar and continue creaming. Add honey gradually and beat until light. Add well-beaten egg. Add dry ingredients and nut meats. Mix well. Form mixture into 2 rolls. Wrap in waxed paper and chill. Slice thin and place on cooky sheets. Bake at 400° F. about 6 to 8 minutes. Yield: 5 dozen cookies.

Honey Nut Brownies

¼ cup shortening, melted
2 squares unsweetened chocolate
1 cup honey
⅝ cup sifted flour
1 teaspoon baking powder
¼ teaspoon salt
¾ cup broken nut meats

To melted shortening add grated chocolate, mix well. Add honey, mix thoroughly. Add sifted dry ingredients and nut meats. Mix well. Pour batter in greased 8-inch square pan. Bake in slow oven (275° F.) about 1 hour. Cut into squares. Yield: 16 two-inch square cookies.

Desserts

Thanksgiving Dinner

Chilled Cranberry and Pineapple Juice
Stuffed Celery   Olives   Salted Nuts
Roast Turkey — Stuffing
Riced Potatoes   Vegetable Tray
Cream Gravy with Almonds and Lightly Flavored with Honey
Hot Rolls
Salad
(Wedges of Grapefruit and Avocado with Pomegranate Seeds. Lemon and Honey Dressing*)
Honey Pumpkin Pie*   Coffee

Baked Honey Prune Whip

1 cup cooked prunes, chopped
2 tablespoons lemon juice
½ teaspoon cinnamon
¼ teaspoon nutmeg
½ cup walnuts, broken
¼ teaspoon salt
3 egg whites
½ cup honey

Combine prunes, lemon juice, spices and nut meats. Add salt to egg whites and beat until stiff. Fold honey in gradually. Fold prune mixture in gradually. Pour into buttered baking dish. Bake in moderate oven (350° F.) about 30 minutes. Serve cold with Honey Cinnamon Sauce.

Honey Cinnamon Sauce

1 tablespoon flour
¼ teaspoon cinnamon
¼ teaspoon salt
¾ cup water
¼ cup honey
1 teaspoon butter

Mix flour, cinnamon, salt. Add water and honey gradually. Cook until thickened, stirring constantly. Add butter. Serve hot.

Sour Cream Honey Pie

1 cup sour cream
2 eggs
¾ cup honey
1 tablespoon flour
1 teaspoon cinnamon
½ teaspoon nutmeg
¼ teaspoon cloves
¼ teaspoon salt
1 cup seeded raisins
½ cup walnuts, broken

Combine ingredients. Pour into 9-inch pastry-lined pan. Bake in hot oven (450° F.) 10 minutes; then bake at 350° F. about 30 minutes, or until mixture will not adhere to knife.

Graham Cracker Upside Down Cake

½ cup butter or margarine
½ cup sugar
½ cup honey
3 eggs, separated
¼ teaspoon salt
2 cups graham cracker crumbs
2½ teaspoons baking powder
½ cup milk
1 teaspoon vanilla
2 tablespoons butter or margarine
4 tablespoons honey
2 large or 3 small eating apples, sliced (or peaches, or bananas)
Cinnamon and nutmeg

Cream butter (or margarine) until soft. Work in sugar gradually and beat well. Add honey, beaten egg yolks and salt. Crush crackers very fine and mix thoroughly with baking powder. Add part of the cracker crumbs to butter mixture. Add remaining crumbs and milk alternately. Add vanilla. Fold in stiffly-beaten egg whites.

Melt 2 tablespoons butter in a large frying pan. Add 4 tablespoons honey. Arrange fruit slices in bottom of large frying pan. Sprinkle lightly with cinnamon and nutmeg. Spoon batter carefully over fruit. Bake in 350° oven 55 to 60 minutes. Loosen around edges and invert on cake rack or plate. May be served warm or cold. Whipped cream sweetened with honey is delicious with this cake.

To crush crackers place on a sheet of waxed paper. Roll with rolling pin. Crumbs may then be poured easily into cup or bowl, by lifting the paper with both hands to form a sort of trough.

Baked Apples with Crumble Topping

3 large apples, cored and cut in halves
5 tablespoons honey
⅔ cup water
2 tablespoons butter
⅛ teaspoon salt
½ teaspoon cinnamon
⅓ cup chopped nut meats
1 cup corn flakes or bran flakes

Arrange apple halves in baking dish and spread each half with 1 teaspoon of the honey. Add enough water to cover bottom of baking dish (about ⅔ cup). Cover and bake in hot oven (400° F.) 20 minutes. Combine butter, remaining 3 tablespoons honey, salt, and cinnamon in sauce pan and mix well. Cook and stir over low heat until mixture bubbles. Add nuts and cereal flakes and mix lightly. Spread cereal mixture over tops of apples. Return to oven and bake, uncovered, 20 minutes longer, or until apples are tender. Yield: 6 servings.

Desserts

Cherry Honey Pie

2 cups pitted cherries
¾ cup honey
3 tablespoons quick-cooking tapioca
1 tablespoon butter
½ teaspoon cinnamon

Combine cherries, honey and tapioca. Pour into 9-inch pastry-lined pan. Dot with butter. Sprinkle with cinnamon. Cover with lattice-top crust. Bake in hot oven (450° F.) 10 minutes. Reduce heat. Bake in moderate oven (350° F.) about 30 minutes.

Pumpkin Chiffon Pie

Crust:

⅓ cup butter
¼ cup honey
½ teaspoon cinnamon
¼ teaspoon nutmeg
1½ cups graham cracker crumbs

Cream butter and honey, add spices, mix well. Add crumbs, mix well. Press mixture on bottom and sides of pie pan or 8 individual pie pans. Bake about 10 minutes at 375° F.

Filling:

1 tablespoon unflavored gelatin
¼ cup cold water
1 cup canned pumpkin
3 eggs, separated
¾ cup honey
1 tablespoon butter
1 cup milk
1 teaspoon cinnamon
½ teaspoon salt
½ teaspoon ginger
¼ teaspoon nutmeg

Soak gelatin in cold water five minutes. Heat pumpkin. Combine beaten egg yolks, honey, butter, milk and spices. Add the pumpkin. Cook in top of double boiler, stirring constantly, about 3 minutes. Add soaked gelatin and stir until gelatin is dissolved. Cool mixture until slightly congealed. Fold in stiffly-beaten whites of eggs. Fill cooked individual pastry shells with mixture. Allow to chill until set.

Honey Custard

2 eggs
¼ cup honey
¼ teaspoon salt
2 cups milk
Grating of nutmeg

Beat eggs slightly. Add honey, salt and scalded milk. Blend well. Pour into custard cups. Sprinkle nutmeg on top. Set cups in pan of warm water and bake at 350° F. about 50 minutes, or until tip of silver knife inserted into custard comes out clean. Yield: 4 servings.

Orange Shortcake

Bake your favorite shortcake. Split while warm and place 4 cups orange sections sweetend with honey between layers and on top. Serve with Honey Orange Sauce.

Honey Orange Sauce

Honey
1 cup orange juice
2 tablespoons grated orange peel

Blend honey into orange juice to sweeten to taste. Add grated orange peel. Blend well. This is an excellent sauce to serve on waffles, hot cakes and French toast as well as on shortcake.

Honey Snow Whip
(A Dessert Sauce)

2 egg whites
2 tablespoons lemon juice
3 tablespoons honey
Dash of salt

Beat egg whites until frothy. Add lemon juice and salt. Continue beating until whites are stiff. Trickle honey over egg whites and beat thoroughly after each addition. If egg whites and honey separate on standing, beat with rotary egg beater and dressing will resume former consistency. Serve with a combination of fresh fruits, Cottage Pudding, Bread Pudding or Steamed Pudding. It lifts everyday desserts into the realm of the clouds.

Fruit Honey Crisp Tarts

½ cup sugar
½ cup honey
¼ teaspoon salt
1 teaspoon vinegar
4 cups crisp rice cereal
2 cups crushed sweetened berries or peaches

Cook sugar and honey together, stirring only enough to prevent burning, to temperature of 270° F. (hard ball in cold water). Remove from heat; add salt and vinegar. Put crisp rice cereal into large buttered bowl; pour in sirup, mixing well. Divide mixture into 4 large buttered tart pans; press evenly against bottom and sides of pans. Cool until firm. Remove tart shells from pans; place on individual serving plates. Fill with fruit. Yield: 4 servings.

Chocolate Meringue Pudding

4 tablespoons cornstarch
¼ teaspoon salt
3 cups milk
⅓ cup honey
2 squares unsweetened chocolate
2 egg yolks, slightly beaten
1 teaspoon vanilla
2 egg whites
4 tablespoons honey

Place cornstarch and salt in top of double boiler, mixing thoroughly. Add milk and honey gradually, stirring well. Add chocolate. Place over boiling water and cook and stir until thickened; then continue cooking 10 minutes, stirring occasionally. Pour small amount of mixture over egg yolks, stirring vigorously; return to double boiler and cook 2 minutes longer. Add vanilla and turn into greased baking dish. Beat egg whites until foamy throughout; add honey, 1 tablespoon at a time, beating after each addition. Then continue beating until mixture will stand in peaks. Pile lightly on chocolate mixture. Bake in moderate oven (350° F.) 10 to 15 minutes, or until delicately browned. Chill. Yield: 6 servings.

Note: Sprinkle meringue with ¼ cup shredded cocoanut before placing in oven if desired.

Chocolate Meringue Pie

½ cup cake flour
½ teaspoon salt
2½ cups milk
½ cup honey
2 squares unsweetened chocolate
3 egg yolks, slightly beaten
2 teaspoons butter or margarine
2 teaspoons vanilla
1 baked 9-inch pie shell
3 egg whites
6 tablespoons honey

Combine flour and salt in top of double boiler. Add milk and honey gradually, stirring well. Add chocolate. Place over boiling water and cook until chocolate is melted and mixture is thick and well blended, stirring constantly. Then continue cooking 10 minutes, stirring occasionally. Pour small amount of mixture over egg yolks, stirring vigorously; return to double boiler and cook 2 minutes longer. Add butter and vanilla. Cool. Turn into pie shell. Beat egg whites until foamy throughout; add honey, 2 tablespoons at a time, beating after each addition until honey is blended. Then continue beating until mixture will stand in peaks. Pile lightly on filling. Bake in moderate oven (350° F.) 10 to 15 minutes, or until delicately browned.

Cereal Party Rings

½ cup honey
¼ cup sugar
½ teaspoon salt
½ tablespoon butter or margarine
6 cups wheat flakes
⅓ cup chopped nut meats, if desired

Combine honey, sugar, and salt and cook 10 minutes or until a small amount of sirup forms a firm ball in cold water (246° F.). Add butter. Add wheat flakes and nuts, stirring lightly to coat flakes. Press into greased ring mold. When cool, unmold and fill center with ice cream, fruit, or fruit-flavored gelatin. Yield: 6 to 8 servings.

Oatmeal Flummery

1½ cups quick-cooking rolled oats
2½ cups boiling water
¾ teaspoon salt
¼ cup honey
¼ cup fruit juice (peach, pineapple, cherry, orange)

Gradually stir rolled oats into boiling water. Add salt. Boil vigorously over direct heat 5 minutes, stirring frequently. Add the honey and fruit juice and mix well. Serve hot with milk. Yield: 4 to 6 servings.

Note: Any left-over canned fruit juice may be used. If sweetened juice is used, reduce honey. One-fourth teaspoon orange juice and one teaspoon grated rind give good flavor.

Farina Pudding

To make pudding from left-over farina, prepare while the farina is still warm; stir in a few tablespoons light cream. To make pudding from freshly-prepared farina, cook according to package directions, substituting an equal amount of milk for water specified. Then sweeten the farina with small amount of honey and flavor with spice (cinnamon, nutmeg, or allspice) or vanilla or almond extract, or grated orange rind. Pour into individual molds; chill until firm and ready to serve. Unmold; arrange nutmeats around base of pudding, pour liquid honey over pudding, sprinkle with spice.

Prize Pudding

Combine 4 cups crisp cereal, ½ cup honey, ¼ cup chopped nut meats and 1 cup diced marshmallows. Pile into shallow casserole; heat in moderate oven (350° F.) about 15 minutes or until marshmallows are slightly melted. Serve hot. Yield: 4 to 6 servings.

Honey Bread Pudding

2½ cups bread cubes
2½ cups milk
4 tablespoons butter
½ cup honey
¼ teaspoon salt
2 eggs
1 teaspoon vanilla extract
½ cup seeded raisins or shredded cocoanut, if desired

Soak bread in milk about 5 minutes. Add butter, honey and salt. Pour mixture gradually over slightly-beaten eggs. Add vanilla. Mix well. Add raisins or cocoanut, if desired. Pour into greased baking dish. Place in a pan of hot water and bake in moderate oven (350° F.) for about 50 minutes, or until firm. Serve with Lemon Sauce.

Lemon Sauce

½ cup honey
1 tablespoon cornstarch
¼ teaspoon salt
1 cup boiling water
Grating of nutmeg
2 tablespoons butter
2 tablespoons lemon juice

Mix honey, cornstarch and salt. Gradually add boiling water and cook over low heat, stirring constantly, until thick and clear. Add nutmeg, butter and lemon juice. Blend well. Serve hot.

Grapefruit Mold

2 tablespoons gelatin
¼ cup cold water
1 cup boiling water
½ cup honey
½ teaspoon salt
1 cup grapefruit juice
½ cup orange juice
¼ cup lemon juice
½ cup chopped walnuts
1 grapefruit

Soak gelatin in cold water 5 minutes; add boiling water and stir until dissolved. Add honey, salt, grapefruit juice, orange juice, and lemon juice, and cool. When mixture is slightly thickened, fold in walnuts and grapefruit segments. Turn mixture into a mold and chill until firm.

Honey Pecan Bavarian

1 package strawberry-flavored gelatin
1½ cups hot water
¼ teaspoon salt
2 teaspoons lemon juice
⅓ cup honey
½ cup light cream
½ cup finely-chopped pecans

Dissolve gelatin in hot water. Add salt, lemon juice and honey. Chill. When slightly thickened, place container in bowl of ice and water and whip with rotary beater until fluffy and thick like whipped cream. Fold in cream and nuts. Turn into mold. Chill until firm. Unmold. Yield: 6 to 8 servings.

Frozen Cranberry Shortcake

1 1-pound can jellied cranberry sauce
½ teaspoon grated orange rind
2 tablespoons honey
1 teaspoon vanilla
2 eggs
2 tablespoons honey
1 cup heavy cream
1 sponge cake

Mix cranberry sauce, orange rind, honey, vanilla and egg yolks. Beat with rotary beater until smooth. Beat egg whites stiff, gradually adding 2 tablespoons honey. Fold into cranberry mixture. Fold in whipped cream. Line freezing tray with waxed paper; then with slices of sponge cake. Pour in cranberry mixture. Top with whipped cream. Freeze. Yield: 6 to 8 servings.

Cranberry Peach Cocktail Freeze

1½ cups canned whole cranberry sauce
½ cup canned peach sirup
¼ cup strained lemon juice
½ cup honey
¼ teaspoon salt
8 servings sliced canned peaches

Press cranberry sauce through strainer. Combine with remaining ingredients; pour into refrigerator tray and freeze until mushy, stirring occasionally. Serve in stemmed glasses over canned peaches. Yield: 8 servings.

Honey Ice Cream

2 cups milk
¾ cup honey
¼ teaspoon salt
2 eggs
1 cup cream

Scald 2 cups whole milk, add honey and salt. Beat eggs. Pour scalded milk into the egg mixture and stir until well blended. Return to double boiler and cook for three or four minutes. Cool. Beat cream and fold into custard mixture. Freeze in refrigerator. Stir once or twice while freezing.

Meats & Vegetables

Christmas Dinner
Tomato Juice
Appetizers
Honey-Glazed Baked Ham*   Maraschino Cherry Garnish
Fluffed Mashed Potatoes   Buttered Broccoli
Honeyed Cranberries in
Green Pepper Cups
Rolls   Butter
Holiday Salad
(Sections of grapefruit and cinnamon apples)
Cheese Tray — Fruit
Coffee

Honeyed Apple Rings

2 large apples
1 cup honey
¼ cup water
1 tablespoon lemon juice
2 sticks cinnamon
4 whole cloves

Wash and core apples. Cut crosswise into 4 slices each. Place in baking dish. Mix honey, water, vinegar and add spices. Pour over apples. Bake uncovered in a moderate oven (375° F.) 30 to 40 minutes.

Honey-Glazed Baked Ham

Place ham, fat side up, on a rack in an open pan. Do not add water. Do not cover. Roast in a preheated low oven (325° F.).

Size	Cooking Time	Approx. Min. Per Pound
16 to 18 lbs.	4 to 4½ hours	15
12 to 15 lbs.	3½ to 4 hours	17
10 to 12 lbs.	3 to 3½ hours	18
8 to 10 lbs.	2¾ to 3 hours	20
5 to 7 lbs.	2 to 2½ hours	22

Remove rind if ham has not had skin removed. Score in diamond shapes. Place ¼ of a maraschino cherry in center of each diamond. Pour 1 cup honey over scored ham. Use more honey if necessary to cover ham uniformly. Bake in a hot oven (400° F.) 15 minutes, or until well browned.

Bananas Baked in Honey

6 bananas
½ cup honey
1 tablespoon lemon juice
1 tablespoon butter
¼ teaspoon salt

Dip bananas in honey and lemon juice. Dot with butter. Sprinkle with salt. Bake in a moderate oven (350° F.) for 15 minutes. Serve as an accompaniment to broiled fish or pork chops.

Orange Honeyed Ham

1 ham
Whole cloves
1 tablespoon grated orange peel
1 cup orange juice
1 cup honey

Place ham, fat side up, in uncovered roaster. Bake in slow oven (300° F.) 25 to 30 minutes per pound. 45 minutes before ham is done remove rind and pour off most of fat in pan. Score the surface in diagonal lines with a sharp knife. Decorate with whole cloves. Blend the grated peel, orange juice and honey. Spread mixture over surface of ham. Return to oven and baste frequently with mixture in pan. Remove from oven when ham is glazed and brown.

Honey Beets

2 tablespoons butter or margarine
½ tablespoon cornstarch
¼ cup lemon juice
2 tablespoons water
½ cup honey
½ teaspoon salt
12 medium-size beets

Melt butter or margarine and blend in cornstarch. Gradually stir in lemon juice, water and honey. Stir until mixture boils and begins to thicken. Boil about 2 minutes, stirring continually. Add salt. Add beets and heat thoroughly. Serve hot. Yield: 6 servings.

Glazed Onions or Carrots

Cook small white onions or carrots in boiling salted water about 20 to 30 minutes, or until tender. Drain. Let stand a few minutes to dry. Melt four tablespoons butter in pan. Add ¼ cup honey. When well blended, add onions or carrots and cook slowly until browned and well glazed. Turn vegetables occasionally for an even glaze.

Candied Sweet Potatoes

Boil 6 medium-size sweet potatoes without paring them. When tender, drain and remove the skins. Cut in half lengthwise and arrange in a buttered baking dish. Season with salt. Heat ¼ cup butter, ½ cup honey, ½ cup orange juice, add to potatoes. Bake in quick oven (400° F.) until potatoes are brown.

Salads

Honey Waffle Supper
Fruit Salad
Cheese Sticks   Olives
Waffles — Honey
Coffee

Golden Salad Dressing

2 eggs, slightly beaten
¼ cup honey
¼ cup lemon juice
½ cup orange juice
Dash of salt

Combine ingredients and cook in double boiler until thickened, stirring frequently. Chill. If desired, just before serving fold in ½ cup cream, whipped. Serve with fruit salads. Yield: About 1 cup.

Sweet-Sour Dressing

4 slices bacon
¼ cup honey
⅓ cup vinegar
1 teaspoon salt
Dash of pepper

Dice bacon, brown. Remove bacon to bowl. Add remaining ingredients to bacon fat. Heat to boiling. Add browned bacon and pour over lettuce or cooked cabbage.

Honey French Dressing
(Delicious on Fruit Salads)

½ cup lemon juice
½ cup honey
½ cup salad oil
1 teaspoon salt

Shake in bottle or jar to blend ingredients. Shake again before serving.

Variation:
Crumble with a fork ¼ pound of Roquefort cheese into small pieces. Add to 1 cup of Honey French Dressing.

Honey-Lemon Dressing

¼ cup honey
¼ cup lemon juice

Blend honey and lemon juice. Serve on fruit salad.

Butterfly Salad

Use date stuffed with cottage cheese for body. Make wings of halves of pineapple slices, decorated with pomegranate seeds or pieces of cherries or berries. Use thin strips of green pepper for antennae. Serve with Honey-Lemon Dressing.

Honey Celery Seed Dressing
(Delicious on Fruit or Vegetable Salads)

1 teaspoon dry mustard
1 teaspoon salt
½ teaspoon paprika
½ cup honey
1 cup salad oil
¼ cup vinegar
1 teaspoon grated onion
1 tablespoon celery seed

Mix dry ingredients in mixing bowl. Add honey and blend well. Add oil and vinegar alternately, beating well with rotary egg beater after each addition. Add onion and celery seed. Yield: About 1⅔ cups dressing.

Cheese Dressing for Fruit Salads

3 ounces cream cheese
2 tablespoons honey
1 tablespoon lemon juice
⅛ teaspoon paprika
½ teaspoon salt
¼ cup orange juice

Soften cream cheese. Add honey and lemon juice and blend well. Add salt and paprika. Add orange juice gradually. Stir until smooth. Yield: About ¾ cup dressing.

Sour Cream Dressing

½ cup thick sour cream
1 tablespoon vinegar
1 teaspoon salt
3 tablespoons honey

Combine ingredients and beat with rotary egg beater until thick.

Cabbage Salad with Sour Cream Dressing

1 cup chilled sour cream
⅓ cup vinegar
½ cup honey
1 teaspoon salt
¼ teaspoon paprika
¼ teaspoon celery salt
½ teaspoon salt
3 cups finely-shredded cabbage

Beat cream until thick. Add vinegar, honey and salt slowly. Beat again for 3 to 4 minutes. Add paprika, celery salt and salt to cabbage. Add sour cream dressing. Mix lightly.

Salads

Sauces

Breakfast

Fresh Berries

Cereal   *Honey*   *Cream*

Omelet   *Bacon*

Muffins   *Honey*

Coffee

Honey Whip for Waffles and Griddle Cakes

¼ cup butter
½ cup honey
½ cup whipped cream

Cream butter thoroughly. Add honey gradually beating well after each addition. Fold in whipped cream.

Honey-Butter Cream

½ cup honey
½ cup evaporated milk
½ cup butter

Combine ingredients. Cook over low heat until mixture forms a smooth sirup, about 10 minutes, stirring frequently. Serve hot or cold. Yield: Sufficient for 12 servings.

Stewed Prunes

1 pound prunes
1 quart water
⅓ cup honey
2 slices lemon

Wash prunes carefully. Put in clean water and let soak overnight. Cook prunes slowly in covered pan in same water they soaked in. Cook until skins are soft. Add honey and lemon juice when prunes are about cooked. Cook apricots in same way.

Apple Sauce

6 tart apples
½ cup honey
½ cup water
1 slice lemon
6 whole cloves

Wash, core, peel and quarter apples. Put honey, water, lemon and cloves in sauce pan. Cook three minutes. Add apples. Cook until tender. Remove cloves and lemon. Yield: 6 servings.

Honey Cream Cheese Topping

1 package (3 ounces) cream cheese
2 tablespoons honey
Dash of salt

Break up cheese with fork. Add honey gradually and beat with fork until well blended. Add salt and mix well. Use as topping for chocolate or spice cake or gingerbread, or serve as a spread on hot muffins or nut bread. Yield: ½ cup topping, or enough to cover top of 10x10x2-inch cake. Use within 4 hours; do not store.

Fluffy Honey Sauce

2 tablespoons honey
½ cup cream, whipped

Fold honey into whipped cream. Use as topping for cake or other desserts. Yield: 1 cup sauce.

Honey Orange Sauce

½ cup honey
3 tablespoons orange juice

Mix honey and orange juice together until blended. Serve on griddle cakes. Yield: ⅔ cup sauce.

Honey Sauce for Ice Cream

4 tablespoons butter
1 tablespoon cornstarch
4 tablespoons cocoa
½ cup honey
½ cup water
6 marshmallows
¼ teaspoon salt
1 teaspoon vanilla extract

Melt butter, add cornstarch and cocoa. Blend well. Add honey and water. Cook over low heat until thick. Add marshmallows and salt. Cook just long enough to melt marshmallows. Add vanilla.

Quick Chocolate Sauce for Ice Cream

½ pound semi-sweet chocolate
½ cup cream
2 tablespoons honey

Melt chocolate in top of double boiler. Gradually add cream and honey beating until smooth.

Chocolate Mint Sauce

1 cup chocolate mints
2 tablespoons honey
½ cup heavy cream

Melt chocolate mints in top of double boiler. Add honey and cream. Beat until smooth.

Honey Specialties

Picnic

Orange Honeyed Baked Ham*	Hard Crust Rolls
Potato Chips	Whole Tomatoes
Pickles	Fudge Cupcakes*
Fresh Fruit	Beverage

Honey and Lemon Juice for Coughs
Equal parts of honey and lemon juice provide a soothing home remedy to relieve throat-tickling coughs.

Honey Tea Biscuits
Bake your favorite baking powder biscuits. When done, remove from oven. Split in halves. Place 1 teaspoon Honey Butter on lower half. Put halves together and let stand a few minutes before serving. To make Honey Butter, cream ¼ cup butter. Add ½ cup honey gradually, creaming mixture well after each addition of honey.

Circus Sandwiches
Make Honey-Peanut Butter (equal parts of Honey Butter and peanut butter) and Honey-Raisin Filling (equal parts of Honey Butter, cream cheese, and chopped seedless raisins) and spread between thin slices of various kinds of bread cut into animal shapes with cooky cutters.

Chicken Cream Gravy lightly flavored with honey with chopped almonds added.

Old Fashioned Fried Apples cooked in honey and butter.

Shoulder Ham baked in honey and apple juice.

Honey Cinnamon Toast
Toast slices of bread on one side. While still hot, butter the untoasted side of bread. Spread buttered side with honey. Sprinkle cinnamon over the top. Place slices under broiler flame until the bread is well browned and the dressing is well blended.

Honey Eggnog on Cereals
Beat two eggs well, gradually add 3 tablespoons honey and two cups milk. Blend thoroughly. Sprinkle with a few grains nutmeg and serve immediately. Yield: Enough for 4 to 6 cereal bowls.

Honey Milk Toast

6 slices bread
Butter
Honey
3 cups hot milk

Toast bread and spread with butter. Place bread in warm bowls. Pour plenty of honey over bread and add the hot milk. Yield: 6 servings.

Broiled Grapefruit

3 grapefruit
12 tablespoons honey
6 maraschino cherries

Wash and cut each grapefruit into halves. Loosen pulp from peel with a sharp knife. Remove seeds and cut out tough fibrous center with scissors. Pour 2 tablespoons honey on each half and place on cold broiler rack set about 4 inches below burner. Broil at 375° F. 15 minutes, or until slightly brown. Garnish each serving with a maraschino cherry. Serve at once. Yield: 6 servings.

Hot Honey Lemonade

1 lemon
2 tablespoons honey
Hot water

Combine juice of lemon and honey in glass. Add enough hot water to fill glass to within 1 inch of top. (Especially good at bed time.)

Honey Cocoa Sirup

1¼ cups cocoa
1 cup sugar
½ teaspoon salt
⅛ teaspoon ground allspice
⅛ teaspoon ground cinnamon
1½ cups boiling water
½ cup honey
2 teaspoons vanilla extract

Combine cocoa, sugar, salt and spices. Add boiling water. Blend. Place over low heat, bring to a boil and boil 5 minutes, stirring constantly. Remove from fire. Cool. Add honey and vanilla. Store in covered jar in refrigerator until ready to use. Yield: Approximately 2¼ cups. *To serve:* Heat ¼ cup Honey Cocoa Sirup with 2 cups scalded milk over boiling water. Before serving, beat with rotary beater. Yield: 3 servings.

Honeyed Cranberry Relish

2 cups fresh cranberries
1 orange
1 cup honey

Pick over and wash cranberries. Wash and quarter orange. Put orange and cranberries through food chopper. Add honey and mix well. Let stand overnight. Chill before serving.

INDEX

APPETIZERS

All Year Fresh Fruit Cup	51
Cheese Bowl	52
Melon Ball Cocktail	51
Pineapple Winter Cocktail	52

BEVERAGES

Coffee	3
Fruit Punch	56
Grape Juice	4
Honey Cocoa Sirup	3
Honeyed Fruit Punch	53
Honey Eggnog	4
Honey Nog Punch Bowl	56
Hot Chocolate	53
Iced Coffee	54
Iced Tea	54
Lemonade	3
Lemon Honeyade	54
Milk	4
Mulled Cider	55
Orange Honeyade	54
Party Punch	55
Refreshing Party Drink	4
Russian Tea	4
Spiced Tea	55
Tea	3

BREADS

Bran Raisin Muffins	10
Christmas Bread	61
Corn Bread	6
Corn Muffins	10
Corn Sticks	61
Date Nut Bread	60
Enriched Bread	5
Fruited Coffee Square with Cranberry Topping and Streusel	57
Holiday Bread	59
Honey Cinnamon Toast	9
Honey Currant Cake	7
Honey Flake Gems	61
Honey French Toast	9
Honey Kuchen	58
Honey Milk Toast	9, 99
Honey Muffins with Variations	10
Honey Oatmeal Bread	6
Honey Orange Muffins	9
Honey Orange Rolls	59
Honey Rolls	8
Honey Topping	8
Hot Cross Buns	58
Nut Bread	6
Orange Nut Bread	6
Pecan Rolls	7
Quick Coffee Cake	8
Refrigerator Rolls	7, 60
Sweet Biscuits	60
Sweet Rolls	8
Waffles	9
Whole Wheat Bread	5

CAKES

All Honey Chocolate Cake	69
Applesauce Cake	15
Brownstone Front Cake	64
Cherry Nut Loaf Cake	72
Chocolate Honey Angel Food Cake	11, 72
Duchess Cake	71
Everyday Cake	15

101

Every Day Honey Cake	67
Fruit Cake	73
Fruited Honey Wedding Cake	63
Fudge Nut Cake	68
Ginger Bread	17
Gold Cake	16
Honey Angel Food Cake	11, 70
Honey Devil's Food Cake (Red)	66
Honey Fruit Cake	13, 71
Honey Fudge Cake	67
Honey Fudge Cupcakes	70
Honey Ginger Cake	13, 65
Honey Layer Cake	14
Honey Nut Cake	64
Honey Orange Cake	66
Honey Sour Cream Spice Cup Cakes	16
Honey Spice Cake	65
Loaf Cake	15
Nut Cake	16
Orange Honey Cake	12
Spice Cake	17
Super Delicious Chocolate Cake	12
Tutti Frutti Cake	17

CANDIES

Candy Roll	22
Caramel Apples	74
Chocolate-Topped Toffee	76
Cream Candy	20
Fruit Candy	21
Honey Bittersweets	19
Honey Caramels	19
Honey Divinity	19
Honeyed Fruit Strips	21
Honey Fondant	19
Honey Fudge	18, 76
Honey-Glazed Pecans	74
Honey Marshmallows	21
Honey Nougat	74
Honey Penuche	20
Honey Popcorn Balls	20
Honey Scotch	75
Honey Squares	22
Honey Taffy	19
Honey Twists	21
Nougat	22
Peanut Brittle	22
Popcorn Balls	75
Spiced Honey Nuts	20
Stuffed Dates	75
Super Delicious Caramels	22

CONFITURES

Beet Pickles	78
Canned Peaches	24
Currant Jelly	23
Fig Preserves	78
Honey Chutney	24
Honey Orange Marmalade	24
Plum Butter	77
Rhubarb Jelly	23, 77
Sunshine Preserves	23
Sweet Fruit Pickles	24

COOKIES

All Honey Cookies	26
Brownies	82
Butter Cookies with Variations	27
Chocolate Chip Cookies	26
Chocolate Fruit Cookies	32
Chocolate Pecan Squares	32
Christmas Cookies	29
Christmas Fruit Nuggets	29
Christmas Honey-Ginger Cookies	30
Date Peanut Butter Drops	31
Eggless Honey Cookies	31
Everyday Cookies	25
Fig Newtons	25
Fruit-Filled Cookies	79
Hermits	26
Honey Bars	28

Honey Cakes	32
Honey Chocolate Chip Cookies	82
Honey Chocolate Chip Squares	81
Honey Chocolate Cookies	83
Honey Drop Cookies	83
Honey Drops	80
Honey Fruit Cookies	81
Honey Gingernuts	28
Honey Icebox Cookies	82
Honey Jam Bars	31
Honey Nut Brownies	28, 83
Honey Nut Cookies	30
Honey Oatmeal Cookies	30, 81
Honey Peanut Butter Cookies	30, 83
Honey Peanut Cookies	32
Honey Peanut Rocks	28
Honey Pecan Cookies	26
Honey Raisin Bars	80
Lebkuchen	29, 80
Lemon Honey Drop Cookies	79
Peanut Butter Brownies	31
Pecan Butterballs	27
Raisin Honey Gems	27

DESSERTS

American Pudding	37
Apple Pie	35
Baked Apples with Crumble Topping	85
Baked Apple with Honey Filling	34
Baked Honey Prune Whip	84
Banbury Tarts	39
Berry Pie	36
Broiled Grapefruit	33, 99
Cereal Party Rings	89
Cherry Honey Pie	86
Chiffon Pie	36
Chocolate Meringue Pie	88
Chocolate Meringue Pudding	88
Coventry Tartlets	39
Cranberry Peach Cocktail Freeze	91
Cranberry Pudding	38
Deep-Dish Apple Pie	36
Farina Pudding	89
French Apple Dumpling with Sauce	39
Frozen Cranberry Shortcake	91
Fruit Honey Crisp Tarts	87
Fruit Rice Ring	37
Graham Cracker Upside Down Cake	85
Grapefruit Mold	90
Honey Apple Crisp	34
Honey Baked Pears	33
Honey Bread Pudding	90
Honey Cinnamon Sauce	84
Honey Custard	37, 86
Honey Delight	37
Honeyed Apples and Cranberries	33
Honey Hard Sauce	37
Honey Ice Cream	34, 91
Honey Orange Sauce	87
Honey Parfait	40
Honey Pecan Bavarian	90
Honey Peppermint Ice Cream	34
Honey Raisin Pie	35
Honey Sauce	38
Honey Snow Whip	87
Honey Steamed Pudding with Sauce	38
Ice Cream Sundae	34
Lemon Sauce	90
Marguerites	34
Oatmeal Flummery	89
Orange Shortcake	87
Pastry	35
Peach Pie	35
Pecan Pie	36
Prize Pudding	89

Pumpkin Chiffon Pie	36, 86
Pumpkin Pie	35
Rhubarb Brown Betty	40
Rhubarb Medley	40
Rhubarb Tarts with Meringue	40
Rice Pudding	38
Sour Cream Honey Pie	84
Tapioca Cream	39
Tart Pastry	39

FILLINGS

Cream Cheese Sandwich Filling	46
Date Filling	79
Fig Filling	
for Fig Newtons	25
for Honey Layer Cake	14
Fruit Filling	46
Lemon Filling	14
Orange Filling	14

FROSTINGS

Boiled Honey Frosting	12
Easy Fluffy Honey Frosting	69
French Honey-Chocolate Frosting	12
Frosting with Chopped Apricots	13
Honey Almond Frosting	73
Honey Meringue	16
Honeymoon Frosting	63
Honey Orange Icing (Uncooked)	69
Quick Frosting for Cake	65
Special Chocolate Frosting	68
Uncooked Honey Frosting	13

FRUITS AND VEGETABLES

Baked Beans	48
Baked Squash	47
Bananas Baked in Honey	93
Candied Sweet Potatoes	47
Family Beets	48
Glazed Onions or Carrots	47
Honey Beets	93
Honeyed Apple Rings	92
Scalloped Tomatoes	48
Sweet Potato Orange Casserole	48
Sweet Sour Cabbage	47

HONEY HINTS	ix–xv

MEATS

Baked Ham with Honey Glazes	41
Canadian Bacon, Fruited and Honeyed	42
Honey-Glazed Baked Ham	92
Honey Spiced Broiled Ham	42
Lamb Chops with Honey-Mint Sauce	42
Orange Honeyed Ham	93

MENUS

Breakfast	96
Bridge Dessert	53
Buffet Luncheon	77
Children's Party	74
Christmas Dinner	92
Holiday Entertaining	51
Honey Waffle Supper	94
Picnic	98
Sunday Brunch	79
Sunday Dinner	57
Thanksgiving Dinner	84
Wedding Reception	63

SALAD DRESSINGS

Boiled Dressing	45
Cheese Dressing for Fruit Salads	95
French Dressing	44
Fruit Salad Dressing	44

104   Index

Golden Salad Dressing 94
Honey Celery Seed
    Dressing 95
Honey French Dressing 45, 94
Honey-Lemon Dressing 94
Lemon Cream Salad
    Dressing 44
Roquefort Cheese Dressing 44
Salad Dressing for Fruit 45
Sour Cream Dressing 95
Sweet-Sour Dressing 94
Thousand Island Dressing 44

SALADS

Avocado Pear Salad 43
Butterfly Salad 95
Cabbage Salad with Sour
    Cream Dressing 95
Cole Slaw 45
French Salad Bowl 43
Frozen Fruit Salad 45
Fruit Salad 43
Fruit Salad Platter 44
Pear Salad 43
Stuffed Tomato Salad 44

SANDWICHES

Cream Cheese Sandwich 46
Fruit Filling Sandwich 46
Honey Butter Sandwich 46
Rolled Sandwich 46
Tea Sandwich 46
Toasted Tea Sandwich 46

SAUCES

Apple Sauce 96
Chocolate Mint Sauce 97
Fluffy Honey Sauce 97
Honey-Butter Cream 96
Honey Cream Cheese
    Topping 97
Honey-Mint Sauce 42
Honey Orange Sauce 97
Honey Sauce for Ice
    Cream 97
Honey Whip for Waffles
    and Griddle Cakes 96
Quick Chocolate Sauce for
    Ice Cream 97
Raisin Sauce 41
Stewed Prunes 96
Sweet Horseradish Sauce 42

SPECIALTIES

Chicken Cream Gravy 98
Circus Sandwiches 98
Honey and Lemon Juice
    for Coughs 98
Honey Cocoa Sirup 99
Honeyed Cranberry
    Relish 99
Honey Eggnog on Cereals 98
Honey Tea Biscuits 98
Hot Honey Lemonade 99
Old Fashioned Fried
    Apples 98
Shoulder Ham 98

Index 105

A CATALOG OF SELECTED
DOVER BOOKS
IN ALL FIELDS OF INTEREST

A CATALOG OF SELECTED DOVER BOOKS IN ALL FIELDS OF INTEREST

THE ART NOUVEAU STYLE, edited by Roberta Waddell. 579 rare photographs of works in jewelry, metalwork, glass, ceramics, textiles, architecture and furniture by 175 artists—Mucha, Seguy, Lalique, Tiffany, many others. 288pp. 8⅜ × 11¼.
23515-7 Pa. $8.95

AMERICAN COUNTRY HOUSES OF THE GILDED AGE (Sheldon's "Artistic Country-Seats"), A. Lewis. All of Sheldon's fascinating and historically important photographs and plans. New text by Arnold Lewis. Approx. 200 illustrations. 128pp. 9⅜ × 12¼.
24301-X Pa. $7.95

THE WAY WE LIVE NOW, Anthony Trollope. Trollope's late masterpiece, marks shift to bitter satire. Character Melmotte "his greatest villain." Reproduced from original edition with 40 illustrations. 416pp. 6⅛ × 9¼.
24360-5 Pa. $7.95

BENCHLEY LOST AND FOUND, Robert Benchley. Finest humor from early 30's, about pet peeves, child psychologists, post office and others. Mostly unavailable elsewhere. 73 illustrations by Peter Arno and others. 183pp. 5⅜ × 8½.
22410-4 Pa. $3.50

ISOMETRIC PERSPECTIVE DESIGNS AND HOW TO CREATE THEM, John Locke. Isometric perspective is the picture of an object adrift in imaginary space. 75 mindboggling designs. 52pp. 8¼ × 11.
24123-8 Pa. $2.50

PERSPECTIVE FOR ARTISTS, Rex Vicat Cole. Depth, perspective of sky and sea, shadows, much more, not usually covered. 391 diagrams, 81 reproductions of drawings and paintings. 279pp. 5⅜ × 8½.
22487-2 Pa. $4.00

MOVIE-STAR PORTRAITS OF THE FORTIES, edited by John Kobal. 163 glamor, studio photos of 106 stars of the 1940s: Rita Hayworth, Ava Gardner, Marlon Brando, Clark Gable, many more. 176pp. 8⅜ × 11¼.
23546-7 Pa. $6.95

STARS OF THE BROADWAY STAGE, 1940-1967, Fred Fehl. Marlon Brando, Uta Hagen, John Kerr, John Gielgud, Jessica Tandy in great shows—*South Pacific, Galileo, West Side Story*, more. 240 black-and-white photos. 144pp. 8⅜ × 11¼.
24398-2 Pa. $8.95

ILLUSTRATED DICTIONARY OF HISTORIC ARCHITECTURE, edited by Cyril M. Harris. Extraordinary compendium of clear, concise definitions for over 5000 important architectural terms complemented by over 2000 line drawings. 592pp. 7½ × 9⅜.
24444-X Pa. $14.95

THE EARLY WORK OF FRANK LLOYD WRIGHT, F.L. Wright. 207 rare photos of Oak Park period, first great buildings: Unity Temple, Dana house, Larkin factory. Complete photos of Wasmuth edition. New Introduction. 160pp. 8⅜ × 11¼.
24381-8 Pa. $7.50

LIVING MY LIFE, Emma Goldman. Candid, no holds barred account by foremost American anarchist: her own life, anarchist movement, famous contemporaries, ideas and their impact. 944pp. 5⅜ × 8½. 22543-7, 22544-5 Pa., Two-vol. set $13.80

UNDERSTANDING THERMODYNAMICS, H.C. Van Ness. Clear, lucid treatment of first and second laws of thermodynamics. Excellent supplement to basic textbook in undergraduate science or engineering class. 103pp. 5⅜ × 8.
63277-6 Pa. $3.50

THE BOOK OF WOOD CARVING, Charles Marshall Sayers. Still finest book for beginning student. Fundamentals, technique; gives 34 designs, over 34 projects for panels, bookends, mirrors, etc. 33 photos. 118pp. 7¾ × 10⅝. 23654-4 Pa. $3.95

CARVING COUNTRY CHARACTERS, Bill Higginbotham. Expert advice for beginning, advanced carvers on materials, techniques for creating 18 projects—mirthful panorama of American characters. 105 illustrations. 80pp. 8⅜ × 11. 24135-1 Pa. $2.50

300 ART NOUVEAU DESIGNS AND MOTIFS IN FULL COLOR, C.B. Grafton. 44 full-page plates display swirling lines and muted colors typical of Art Nouveau. Borders, frames, panels, cartouches, dingbats, etc. 48pp. 9⅜ × 12¼. 24354-0 Pa. $6.00

SELF-WORKING CARD TRICKS, Karl Fulves. Editor of *Pallbearer* offers 72 tricks that work automatically through nature of card deck. No sleight of hand needed. Often spectacular. 42 illustrations. 113pp. 5⅜ × 8½. 23334-0 Pa. $2.25

CUT AND ASSEMBLE A WESTERN FRONTIER TOWN, Edmund V. Gillon, Jr. Ten authentic full-color buildings on heavy cardboard stock in H-O scale. Sheriff's Office and Jail, Saloon, Wells Fargo, Opera House, others. 48pp. 9¼ × 12¼. 23736-2 Pa. $3.95

CUT AND ASSEMBLE AN EARLY NEW ENGLAND VILLAGE, Edmund V. Gillon, Jr. Printed in full color on heavy cardboard stock. 12 authentic buildings in H-O scale: Adams home in Quincy, Mass., Oliver Wight house in Sturbridge, smithy, store, church, others. 48pp. 9¼ × 12¼. 23536-X Pa. $3.95

THE TALE OF TWO BAD MICE, Beatrix Potter. Tom Thumb and Hunca Munca squeeze out of their hole and go exploring. 27 full-color Potter illustrations. 59pp. 4¼ × 5½. (Available in U.S. only) 23065-1 Pa. $1.50

CARVING FIGURE CARICATURES IN THE OZARK STYLE, Harold L. Enlow. Instructions and illustrations for ten delightful projects, plus general carving instructions. 22 drawings and 47 photographs altogether. 39pp. 8⅜ × 11. 23151-8 Pa. $2.50

A TREASURY OF FLOWER DESIGNS FOR ARTISTS, EMBROIDERERS AND CRAFTSMEN, Susan Gaber. 100 garden favorites lushly rendered by artist for artists, craftsmen, needleworkers. Many form frames, borders. 80pp. 8¼ × 11. 24096-7 Pa. $3.50

CUT & ASSEMBLE A TOY THEATER/THE NUTCRACKER BALLET, Tom Tierney. Model of a complete, full-color production of Tchaikovsky's classic. 6 backdrops, dozens of characters, familiar dance sequences. 32pp. 9⅜ × 12¼. 24194-7 Pa. $4.50

ANIMALS: 1,419 COPYRIGHT-FREE ILLUSTRATIONS OF MAMMALS, BIRDS, FISH, INSECTS, ETC., edited by Jim Harter. Clear wood engravings present, in extremely lifelike poses, over 1,000 species of animals. 284pp. 9 × 12. 23766-4 Pa. $8.95

MORE HAND SHADOWS, Henry Bursill. For those at their 'finger ends," 16 more effects—Shakespeare, a hare, a squirrel, Mr. Punch, and twelve more—each explained by a full-page illustration. Considerable period charm. 30pp. 6½ × 9¼. 21384-6 Pa. $1.95

CATALOG OF DOVER BOOKS

TOLL HOUSE TRIED AND TRUE RECIPES, Ruth Graves Wakefield. Popovers, veal and ham loaf, baked beans, much more from the famous Mass. restaurant. Nearly 700 recipes. 376pp. 5⅜ × 8½. 23560-2 Pa. $4.95

FAVORITE CHRISTMAS CAROLS, selected and arranged by Charles J.F. Cofone. Title, music, first verse and refrain of 34 traditional carols in handsome calligraphy; also subsequent verses and other information in type. 79pp. 8⅜ × 11. 20445-6 Pa. $3.00

CAMERA WORK: A PICTORIAL GUIDE, Alfred Stieglitz. All 559 illustrations from most important periodical in history of art photography. Reduced in size but still clear, in strict chronological order, with complete captions. 176pp. 8⅜ × 11¼. 23591-2 Pa. $6.95

FAVORITE SONGS OF THE NINETIES, edited by Robert Fremont. 88 favorites: "Ta-Ra-Ra-Boom-De-Aye," "The Band Played On," "Bird in a Gilded Cage," etc. 401pp. 9 × 12. 21536-9 Pa. $10.95

STRING FIGURES AND HOW TO MAKE THEM, Caroline F. Jayne. Fullest, clearest instructions on string figures from around world: Eskimo, Navajo, Lapp, Europe, more. Cat's cradle, moving spear, lightning, stars. 950 illustrations. 407pp. 5⅜ × 8½. 20152-X Pa. $4.95

LIFE IN ANCIENT EGYPT, Adolf Erman. Detailed older account, with much not in more recent books: domestic life, religion, magic, medicine, commerce, and whatever else needed for complete picture. Many illustrations. 597pp. 5⅜ × 8½. 22632-8 Pa. $7.95

ANCIENT EGYPT: ITS CULTURE AND HISTORY, J.E. Manchip White. From pre-dynastics through Ptolemies: society, history, political structure, religion, daily life, literature, cultural heritage. 48 plates. 217pp. 5⅜ × 8½. (EBE) 22548-8 Pa. $4.95

KEPT IN THE DARK, Anthony Trollope. Unusual short novel about Victorian morality and abnormal psychology by the great English author. Probably the first American publication. Frontispiece by Sir John Millais. 92pp. 6½ × 9¼. 23609-9 Pa. $2.95

MAN AND WIFE, Wilkie Collins. Nineteenth-century master launches an attack on out-moded Scottish marital laws and Victorian cult of athleticism. Artfully plotted. 35 illustrations. 239pp. 6⅛ × 9¼. 24451-2 Pa. $5.95

RELATIVITY AND COMMON SENSE, Herman Bondi. Radically reoriented presentation of Einstein's Special Theory and one of most valuable popular accounts available. 60 illustrations. 177pp. 5⅜ × 8. (EUK) 24021-5 Pa. $3.50

THE EGYPTIAN BOOK OF THE DEAD, E.A. Wallis Budge. Complete reproduction of Ani's papyrus, finest ever found. Full hieroglyphic text, interlinear transliteration, word-for-word translation, smooth translation. 533pp. 6½ × 9¼. (USO) 21866-X Pa. $8.50

COUNTRY AND SUBURBAN HOMES OF THE PRAIRIE SCHOOL PERIOD, H.V. von Holst. Over 400 photographs floor plans, elevations, detailed drawings (exteriors and interiors) for over 100 structures. Text. Important primary source. 128pp. 8⅜ × 11¼. 24373-7 Pa. $5.95

CATALOG OF DOVER BOOKS

THE PRINCIPLE OF RELATIVITY, Albert Einstein et al. Eleven most important original papers on special and general theories. Seven by Einstein, two by Lorentz, one each by Minkowski and Weyl. 216pp. 5⅜ × 8½. 60081-5 Pa. $3.50

PINEAPPLE CROCHET DESIGNS, edited by Rita Weiss. The most popular crochet design. Choose from doilies, luncheon sets, bedspreads, apron—34 in all. 32 photographs. 48pp. 8¼ × 11. 23939-X Pa. $2.00

REPEATS AND BORDERS IRON-ON TRANSFER PATTERNS, edited by Rita Weiss. Lovely florals, geometrics, fruits, animals, Art Nouveau, Art Deco and more. 48pp. 8¼ × 11. 23428-2 Pa. $1.95

SCIENCE-FICTION AND HORROR MOVIE POSTERS IN FULL COLOR, edited by Alan Adler. Large, full-color posters for 46 films including *King Kong, Godzilla, The Illustrated Man,* and more. A bug-eyed bonanza of scantily clad women, monsters and assorted other creatures. 48pp. 10¼ × 14¼. 23452-5 Pa. $8.95

TECHNICAL MANUAL AND DICTIONARY OF CLASSICAL BALLET, Gail Grant. Defines, explains, comments on steps, movements, poses and concepts. 15-page pictorial section. Basic book for student, viewer. 127pp. 5⅜ × 8½. 21843-0 Pa. $2.95

STORYBOOK MAZES, Dave Phillips. 23 stories and mazes on two-page spreads: *Wizard of Oz, Treasure Island, Robin Hood,* etc. Solutions. 64pp. 8¼ × 11. 23628-5 Pa. $2.25

PUNCH-OUT PUZZLE KIT, K. Fulves. Engaging, self-contained space age entertainments. Ready-to-use pieces, diagrams, detailed solutions. Challenge a robot, split the atom, more. 40pp. 8¼ × 11. 24307-9 Pa. $3.50

THE HUMAN FIGURE IN MOTION, Eadweard Muybridge. Over 4500 19th-century photos showing stopped-action sequences of undraped men, women, children jumping, running, sitting, other actions. Monumental collection. 390pp. 7⅞ × 10⅝. 20204-6 Clothbd. $18.95

PHOTOGRAPHIC SKETCHBOOK OF THE CIVIL WAR, Alexander Gardner. Reproduction of 1866 volume with 100 on-the-field photographs: Manassas, Lincoln on battlefield, slave pens, etc. 224pp. 10⅝ × 8¼. 22731-6 Pa. $6.95

FLORAL IRON-ON TRANSFER PATTERNS, edited by Rita Weiss. 55 floral designs, large and small, realistic, stylized; poppies, iris, roses, etc. Victorian, modern. Instructions. 48pp. 8¼ × 11. 23248-4 Pa. $1.95

AUTOBIOGRAPHY: The Story of My Experiments with Truth, Mohandas K. Gandhi. Boyhood, legal studies, purification, the growth of the man who freed India. 480pp. 5⅜ × 8½. 24593-4 Pa. $6.95

ON THE IMPROVEMENT OF THE UNDERSTANDING, Benedict Spinoza. Also contains *Ethics, Correspondence,* all in excellent R Elwes translation. Basic works on entry to philosophy, pantheism, exchange of ideas with great contemporaries. 420pp. 5⅜ × 8½. 20250-X Pa. $5.95

Prices subject to change without notice.

Available at your book dealer or write for free catalog to Dept. GI, Dover Publications, Inc., 31 East 2nd St. Mineola, N.Y. 11501. Dover publishes more than 175 books each year on science, elementary and advanced mathematics, biology, music, art, literary history, social sciences and other areas.